CHALLENGE™
EVERYTHING

CHALLENGE EVERYTHING™

SCOTT CULLATHER & KRISTINA McCOOBERY

THE BATTLE CRY
THAT BLEW SH*T UP
AND INVNTd
LIVE BRAND STORYTELLING™

ForbesBooks

Published by ForbesBooks, Charleston, South Carolina.
Member of Advantage Media Group.

ForbesBooks is a registered trademark, and the ForbesBooks colophon is a trademark of Forbes Media, LLC.

Printed in the United States of America.

10 9 8 7 6 5 4 3 2

ISBN: 978-1-946633-87-3
LCCN: 2019915863

Cover design by Claude Carril.
Layout design by Wesley Strickland.

This publication is designed to provide accurate and authoritative information in regard to the subject matter covered. It is sold with the understanding that the publisher is not engaged in rendering legal, accounting, or other professional services. If legal advice or other expert assistance is required, the services of a competent professional person should be sought.

Advantage Media Group is proud to be a part of the Tree Neutral® program. Tree Neutral offsets the number of trees consumed in the production and printing of this book by taking proactive steps such as planting trees in direct proportion to the number of trees used to print books. To learn more about Tree Neutral, please visit **www.treeneutral.com**.

Since 1917, the Forbes mission has remained constant. Global Champions of Entrepreneurial Capitalism. ForbesBooks exists to further that aim by bringing the Stories, Passion, and Knowledge of top thought leaders to the forefront. ForbesBooks brings you The Best in Business. To be considered for publication, please visit **www.forbesbooks.com**.

Dedicated to Dan Cullather, the man who taught us much more than tough business lessons.
He taught us the importance of showing up.
Thanks, Dad. Love you.

—Scott and Kristina

ACKNOWLEDGMENTS

Our book tells the story of our eleven-year journey and would not be possible without the hundreds of full-time INVNTrs from around the world, our trusted vendors and freelancers, and our family and friends who have supported us and made us better—in particular the guidance, love, camaraderie, and friendship of Matti Leshem, Carolyn Buck Luce, Gordon Thompson III, John Wringe, Paul Blurton, Jim McDonald, Mike Kitson, Jerry Deeney, Wolf Karbe, Lauren Carril, Laura Roberts, Eva Swedlund, Lynn Cullather, and Doug DeRosa.

TICK TICK TICK BOOM

Once upon a time, or so the story goes, a guy and a girl—we'll call them Adam and Eve—were hanging around butt naked in Paradise. They got mixed up with a no-legged hustler, munched the wrong apple, and before you know it—boom!—Modern civilization.

This is how it all began and how it still begins. With a *great* freakin' story.

From Noah hammering away without a cloud in the sky, to a star-crossed teen couple in fair Verona, all the way through urban legends that have us wary of Bloody Mary and spider bites, our stories help us organize and analyze our human experience. And as we share them, our stories build community, articulate values and identities, circulate big ideas, and plant memorable characters, scenarios, and turns of phrase in our "collective unconscious." Once we had a tribal campfire, later on, a water cooler. And today, live events embody that essential human exchange, where narrative and experience meet. These days there's pervasive anxiety that we're living too much of our lives behind screens. Yet when everyone around the world considers the future of their respective countries, they say two things are essential to promoting positive change: connecting with one another

Has "social technology" really made us less social?

in real life, and the resulting expansion of perspective.[1] The way *we* see it, live events are counterprogramming to that potential and worrisome numbing out. They are the flesh and blood, can't-buy-it, utterly and undeni-

ably *present* beating pulse of our global conversation, connecting the heart, mind, body, and soul to a cause, a mission, a movement, and yes—to brands.

As partners in a global live brand storytelling™ agency, we get asked this one a lot: What's the future of live events? To which we say: "Meet the new CEO." As in, Chief *Experience* Officer. Think about it. In just the last few years, the Chief Human Resources/Chief People Officer has emerged as a strategic role, often reporting directly to the CEO.

When major voices like the *Harvard Business Review*[2] and former Google People Ops leader Laszlo Bock, in his important book *Work Rules*, ignited what's now a familiar discussion about giving the HR function a prominent seat at the executive leadership table, old ideas about HR being strictly concerned with payroll, benefits, and proce-

---

1 Eventbrite, "The Experience Movement: Research Report," accessed October 4, 2019, https://www.eventbrite.com/l/millennialsreport-2017/.

2 Ram Charan, Dominic Barton, Denis Carey, "People Before Strategy: A New Role for the CHRO," *Harvard Business Review*, July–August 2015.

dures soon went the way of the flip phone. Any company gunning for hypergrowth, counting on its millennial and Gen Z workforce, invested in diversity and inclusion, and wanting to recruit, develop, and retain top talent absolutely needs a visionary executive in this essential role. As far as we're concerned, when it comes to a brand's relevance and a company's future, *it's the exact same deal for live events.*

Plain and simple: Events aren't campaign extensions anymore. They're not the free gift with purchase or the cherry on top. *They're everything.* And companies that don't have an event engagement or experience strategy—and a role dedicated to the craft in their C-suites—without question are going to fail.

Why? Because the counterpoint to the ever-rising prominence of our relationship to devices such as smartphones, smart watches, and tablets is our urgent and pervasive craving for real, live human connections. In fact, the more time we spend engaged with technology, the more our innate need to connect, driven by our foundational wiring otherwise known as the human condition, seeks satisfaction. It's unsurprising, then, that 74 percent of Americans now prioritize experiences over products.[3] The ideal modern state is *phygital*—a simultaneous mode that traverses our online and offline worlds and identities.

Additionally, millennials and Gen Zers, the generations who'd rather spend their money on experiences than "things,"[4] make up 2.43 billion and 2.46 billion respectively—or well over half of the

---

3   Blake Morgan, "NOwnership, No Problem: An Updated Look At Why Millennials Value Experiences Over Owning Things," Forbes, January 2, 2019, https://www.forbes.com/sites/blakemorgan/2019/01/02/nownership-no-problem-an-updated-look-at-why-millennials-value-experiences-over-owning-things/#45559a05522f.

4   Eventbrite, "The Experience Movement: Research Report,"accessed October 4, 2019, https://www.eventbrite.com/l/millennialsreport-2017/.

world's population of over 7.7 billion people.[5] This figure is expected to grow, while this powerhouse demographic will simultaneously rise in professional ranking and earning power. Brands that want to engage them meaningfully must meet them where they live, and where they care.

But don't take our word for it. According to *Fast Company*, experience economy spending is rising exponentially, and predicted to reach $8 trillion by 2030.[6]

Which brings us to why we wrote this book.

We're sharing our story, our tools, and some critical lessons we've learned along the way because we firmly believe it's an abundant universe, with more than enough for all of us. With over fifty collective years of experience in designing and producing live events and experiential campaigns all over the world, we've built a global agency and invented live brand storytelling. Our business is fueled by collaboration. Chances are, if you picked up this book, yours is, too—whether you're an engaged CEO, a seasoned CMO, successful CRO, or a recent grad looking for context and strategy as you enter this remarkable space. As each of our interconnected endeavors expands and succeeds, it's good news for all of us.

We invite you to apply our tools to energize your live event conception and execution. From there, you can harness the undeniable *power of live* and use it to take your projects, partnerships, and performance to the next level.

---

5   Lee J. Miller and Wei Lu, "Gen Z Is Set to Outnumber Millennials Within a Year," Bloomberg, August 20, 2018, https://www.bloomberg.com/news/articles/2018-08-20/ gen-z-to-outnumber-millennials-within-a-year-demographic-trends.

6   Claire Miller, "Why Airbnb, Target, and Walmart are betting on the experience economy," *Fast Company*, August 5, 2019, https://www.fastcompany.com/90378285/ why-airbnb-target-and-walmart-are-betting-on-the-experience-economy.

In the first part of our book, we'll take you on the wild ride that got us here. (You'll surely observe in our tale both what to do and what *not* to do.) In the second half of the book, we'll take a deeper dive into "The Work," sharing the proprietary creative process that has delivered us extraordinary results countless times. We think they'll work wonders for you, too.

We're glad you're here. Because here, the only place to be, is *exactly* where live events happen.

And man, do we want you to crush it.

PART ONE

THE
STORY

CHAPTER 1

WHY INVNT?

You're in a roller coaster with your best friend, and you're riding up that first hill. You bought your ticket and waited in line, and now there's just the tick, tick, tick, as you lurch skyward. You're thinking: Holy shit. You grab hands, and grin at each other: "We're doing this." And in the split second that you reach the very top, you both holler: "F**k! Are we really doing this?" Oh, yeah. We're doing this. That's what it was like.

–Scott Cullather

Want to be an entrepreneur?
Get ready for a wild, unpredictable ride!

t's a clear summer morning in 2008. We've got a global economic meltdown on our hands, with daily reminders that the marketing communications sector is a leading economic indicator (typically the first in line for budget cuts, and the last to come back); other than all that, we're feeling good. A little nervous, but good. Scott's flight to Chicago is uneventful, and now he's headed to the meeting to which our bosses have invited him, as prepared and fired up as a guy can get. Kristina is standing by in New York, already proud of the big move that's been thoughtfully crafted over many months. It's just a matter of slipping the keys into the ignition and driving our big, beautiful, totally sensical future straight off the lot.

Except the universe is telling our story. And the universe has a very, very different idea about how this whole thing's gonna go.

We'd met at work several years before, at the esteemed agency Williams/Gerard, worked closely together, and fallen in love. We were clearly an effective business partnership. In lockstep, we'd built our employer's largest, most profitable office, with a substantial head count. We had the biggest, most high-profile accounts. Our downtown New York City office was humming. And we were deeply aligned on the soul level, too. Four months earlier, we'd moved in together, into a sunny, tiny but charming rental apartment on Manhattan's Upper West Side, and now we were blending our families together. Three lively, whip smart little kids, Caitlin, Christian, and Mia, all adopted, in kindergarten and second grade at the time.

It was a lot. But a *good* kind of a lot.

Among the many things we agreed on was that our employer's business model wasn't scalable or sustainable. With only two of the five original shareholders left—guys who'd founded the company forty-five years earlier, now in their sixties and seventies—there was

A young Scott with his dad, Dan, and American "Rat Pack" legend Sammy Davis Jr.

no clear path forward. Heck, other than a paycheck, there wasn't even a reason to care. Except we *did* care. We cared because Scott had grown up in the business, getting the bug at an early age and building his career there over eighteen years. His father, Dan Cullather, a pioneer in the live events industry and the thirteenth employee at Jack Morton Worldwide (now owned by Interpublic Group), who'd retired two years earlier, had been a partner. And Kristina had a decade with the agency under her belt. Objectively speaking, we perceived that a certain uninventiveness had begun to settle over the agency, if not the industry at large. We knew that something had to change. (Spoiler alert! That change, turns out, was *us!*) But subjectively, we had feelings for the place. The business was Scott's home. His father's legacy.

The two remaining Founders of Williams/Gerard didn't have a vision for its growth or evolution. There was no succession plan. No exit strategy for themselves or the agency's leadership. And that gap clearly presented to us an amazing opportunity to step in as the next generation of leaders.

Working together over several months, we began to develop a transition plan, refreshed business model, and exit strategy for the Founders so that we could take over the business and send its elder statesmen into the sunset with a rich retirement plan worthy of their collective lifetime of effort. We began what seemed to be promising talks with Williams/Gerard leadership. We were excited. There we were, hired employees without an ounce of stock in the company, only as good as our last project, now poised to take the helm. To be able to give back to the folks who'd taught us so much, to offer them a sound retirement plan with the promise that what they'd built would continue and expand, to run the entire company the way we were running the New York office, installing the best and the brightest and growing the presence of women in leadership roles. Would there be a negotiation? Of course. Might it get tricky? Sure. But all of this was adding up to VERY COOL.

Which brings us back to that breezy summer morning on Wabash Avenue in Chicago—Williams/Gerard HQ—for what Scott assumes will be a fruitful continuation of those talks. "Close the door," Scott's boss, one of the two remaining partners, instructs when Scott arrives at the conference room on the fifth floor. "This is going to be a very difficult conversation." Producing a folder, they unfurl a twelve-page memo that announces a ninety-day leave of absence to address Scott's purported "insubordination," as well as a slew of harrowing accusations that don't remotely reflect reality as we know it.

These gentlemen, Scott's father's former business partners for over forty years, whom Scott has known since childhood, explain that during his leave, Scott is forbidden to speak to any vendors, clients, or employees, including Kristina. So, Scott does what any red-blooded individual would do under these surreal circumstances: he smiles politely. And then he gets up from the table.

"Thank you very much," Scott says, offering handshakes. "Have a great summer."

One of the partners seems puzzled. "You don't wanna talk about this at all?"

"Nope. I'd say it's pretty clear."

At the elevator, Scott's informed that members of the Williams/Gerard executive team have already been dispatched to the New York office to announce Scott's news before he has a chance to share it himself. Thanks to a flight delay, Scott reaches Kristina and beats them to it. Pulling up at O'Hare airport, the taxi driver announces that Scott's corporate AMEX has been declined. At check-in, Scott learns that his return ticket to New York has been cancelled.

Talk about a parting gift.

On the plane, a devastated Scott calls his dad to break the news, only to learn that the remaining partners have already reported to Dan their claims against Scott. There was certainly a bit of uncertainty in the beginning, Dan hearing two very different stories from Scott and his former business partners. Meanwhile, back in New York City, Kristina launches into "fix it" mode. "This is not over," she tells herself. "They've made a terrible decision. They have no idea what they've done." She just wants a chance to *speak* with them, so that she can undo all of it. She's informed that security has been called, on the chance that Scott might "go postal." Her mind racing, she considers the dual senior management meeting events on the docket for the next few weeks, for PepsiCo and SC Johnson, respectively, and the integral role that Scott has played with these key accounts.

"You realize," Kristina says to the partners who effectively just terminated Scott, "that you've made a colossal mistake that will destroy the business." It's rapidly dawning on her that some of the people she and Scott trusted most have been—chillingly—part of the coup.

"It's *your* book of business," they reply. "Figure it out."

And over the course of that very same, very long night, we began to do just that.

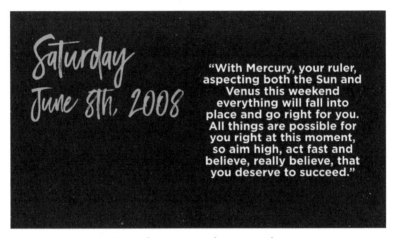

Scott's horoscope on that very night.
Spookily accurate.

> Entrepreneur: A person who starts a business and is willing to risk loss in order to make money.
>
> **–Merriam-Webster Dictionary**

First thing Monday morning, we sit down with highly recommended labor attorney Andrew Bernstein, who's become a family friend and still offers us advice and guidance today. Andrew points out the positive implications of having no contracts and no noncompete stipulations. "If you really want to start your own business," Andrew tells Scott, "then you need to follow my instructions implicitly then go Jerry Fu**king Maguire on them and take everything." By end of day Scott resigns and comes up with a shitty name for the new agency, Oculus. Thankfully, gifted brand guru, Matti Leshem, who recently founded a successful Hollywood film company with his wife Lynn, Weimaraner Republic Pictures, and to this day is still one of our dearest friends, quickly comes up with a better one.

Of course, we consider naming the venture we're birthing after ourselves, like any proud parents would. But we're also learning giant, painful lessons at warp speed: whatever we're creating, we want it to be scalable and sustainable. A venture that will survive long after us. Talk about blowing shit up—it feels like our *lives* have just been destroyed. And from those shattered but still bright shards, we want to shake up the live event industry with a new kind of agency model, attitude, culture, and results-driven approach. Talented graphic designer Nils Swedlund (who also

INVNT's original logo, which has since evolved.

happens to be Kristina's brother) designs our first INVNT logo. On Tuesday INVNT is incorporated and Scott's new business cards arrive. With the ink still drying he indeed goes "postal," but not according to his former agency's concerns. Every single account he and Kristina had led is now officially fair game—and Scott's going in.

First, PepsiCo, then SC Johnson, Merck, Subway ... to a one, these major clients say, "We don't know who Williams or Gerard are—we know Scott and Kristina. As long as it's legal, and you can get through procurement, we're going with you." The phone starts ringing off the hook with the many folks from our former agency who want to join us. Scott's dad, Dan, realizes quickly that what he's been told isn't the truth. He becomes a beloved mentor and the biggest cheerleader we have. To this day, he's the first person we call for advice.

Three weeks later, news of Scott's departure is openly circulating on the industry grapevine. Kristina does her best to remain a loyal employee while managing reactions. "Are you fucking kidding me?" one of our biggest clients says to her. "Nobody's said a thing to us." Back at Williams/Gerard, they're apparently pretending that Scott is still on the team. "Doing this project without Scott is like watching *Indiana Jones* without Harrison Ford. We want out of our contract."

INVNT's first company meeting consists of our entire team of five people around our dining room table in our apartment, psyching ourselves up to rock the world, deeply grateful and indebted to our first three clients, all of whom have left Williams/Gerard to follow us, trying not to freak out over *The New York Times* headline that hollers "U.S. economy generally 'weak,' Fed reports." [7] Within that same year, we open up a second office in DC. By the following year, we grow to $10 million, opening up a third office in Detroit. By 2010, we have $20 million in revenue.

Today INVNT's eight offices are located in key cities all over the globe.

---

7   "U.S. economy 'generally weak,' Fed reports," *The New York Times*, June 11, 2008.

Today INVNT has eight offices in five countries on four continents across six time zones, with revenues in excess of $65 million and an impressive team of over one hundred wicked smart teenagers (and we'll tell you what we mean by that very soon)—each of whom agrees not to take our IP, confidential information, client relationships, or employees!

The Williams/Gerard agency we knew sadly closed its doors in 2018, handing so many talented employees, without warning, a terrible fate as a result. We offer thanks to each and every person and experience associated with our time at Williams/Gerard, for leading us to more personal and professional fulfillment than we could ever have dreamed of. To those of you who were there for us and continue to be supportive friends, colleagues, and competitors, we are forever grateful.

TAKEAWAY:
THE END IS THE BEGINNING

The moment of absolute certainty will never come.
Don't wait for it.

–Kristina McCoobery

We promised you a wild ride, and it sure makes a great story, doesn't it?

But honestly, the way we did it is *really* not the way to do it.

Had Scott not been fired from Williams/Gerard, we'd probably still be there today. Who knows? Maybe Williams/Gerard wouldn't have gone out of business if we'd stayed. We also like to fantasize about what life would have been like if we'd grown a pair. (Or, a pair of pairs.) If we'd quit, instead of trying to make it work and getting booted from the nest, hard.

Had we *planned* to compete, we could have arrived at our crossroads much better prepared, with a better financial plan. "Fake it till you make it" is great copy, but living that way brings with it many, many sleepless nights; our "plan" was taking every single penny we had and throwing it into the business. And by "every single penny," that's exactly what we mean. Our entire life savings was on the line. We'd cashed out our 401(k)s and maxed out every credit card. We weren't kids cooking up a big idea in our parents' garage: we were parents ourselves, of three young kids, no less. And we really and truly had *zero idea* whether the tremendous risk we'd undertaken, and the tremendous pressure we were under, was going to have anything resembling an upside. Having lived through it all, it makes complete sense to us that 90 percent of start-ups fail[8]—we're kind of surprised that number isn't higher! Eleven years on, we're well aware that some perceive our lives as glamorous. Yes, we have a few fancy things and we'd be disingenuous at best not to own our comfortable lifestyle. But without a doubt we're working as hard as we ever did. Logging a sometimes gruelling travel schedule to stay connected and present with our clients and teams across the globe. Rolling up our sleeves and participating rigorously in the design and execution of pitches. Overseeing key projects. And constantly engaged in strategy as we continue to scale, sustainably.

Recently, an INVNTr who came on board six or seven years into the company's life gave us a sigh and a smile. "You know," this talented, hardworking, capable person said, "sometimes I wish I'd been with you guys back in the very

8   Griffith, Erin, "*Why Start-ups Fail, According to Their Founders,*" *Fortune,* September 25, 2014. https://fortune.com/2014/09/25/ why-startups-fail-according-to-their-founders/.

beginning. I wish we could have taken this entire journey together." We love the sentiment, but when we told her about all the sacrifices and risks we had to take during that first chapter of our success story, she changed her mind. "Trust us," we assured her. "Now is better."

But don't let us scare you away. If you're poised for growth and expansion, if you see the writing on the wall, if your heart of hearts is speaking to you loudly, here's some advice to chew on.

READY TO TAKE THE LEAP? HERE'S WHAT TO DO

- **Plan to Compete.** Maybe you can't compete because of your contract. But that doesn't mean you can't *plan* to. Don't just sit there stewing in what you already know. You are your own exit strategy.

- **It's Who You Know.** Look around your office, your inbox, and your circle. Construct your dream team of creative partners and legal/financial advisors based on the super awesome geniuses with whom you already do your best work. (And ask them for attorney references if you don't already have that covered.) These are the people you're taking with you. For now, forget about what you're going to call yourselves, who's designing the logo, or which espresso machine communicates your mission statement. In our industry, the people are the whole point.

- **Resign.** That's right, you heard us. If you're unhappy and you know it, get "the hell out of Dodge." Go out on your own or take a breather and regroup.

- **Go Jerry F**king Maguire.** We're not saying break the law, because you're way too talented to get waylaid in legal proceedings. But if you built the campaign, if you brought in the business, if you manage the relationship and the account … don't just slink into the night when you go. Let each and every one of your clients know (preferably at the last minute and from your personal phone or computer to sidestep fallout). If your lawyer says it's okay, contact your clients after you leave, and if at all possible take them with you. Who knows? They might even choose to follow you.

- **IP Is Your Superpower.** Besides its people, the biggest asset any service-driven business has is its intellectual property. Our name may be INVNT, but we don't invent hardware or software—we invent ideas and brand positioning, both of which, turns out, are just as stealable and replicable as patented "stuff." So anytime we have the opportunity to actually trademark or register, we spend the money and do it. *And we strongly recommend this to every one of you.* The value of this practice is worth its weight in gold, because IP is a key differentiator that nobody else can claim. Don't just make great shit. Own it!

Your ideas are your IP. Safeguard them by trademarking and registering them.

- **If you start your own thing, get every single employee to sign a contract.** Don't be naïve! If you took all your marbles with you when you left, you know exactly how it's done. If you don't want it done to you, you must set healthy and professional boundaries with your team.

WHAT NOT TO DO

- **Never, ever underestimate your people.** We were severely underestimated. They never saw us coming. "We're not really worried about Kristina," a former colleague said. "She's a single mom, she's got a little kid in private school—she's not going anywhere." Hearing that, especially the thick layer of sexism on top of the condescension, only fueled Kristina's determination to leave, taking every piece of business she could. In fact, even years later, if there was a small account floating out there and we knew it was theirs, we would just go after it, guns blazing.

WHAT'S NEXT

In the next chapter, we'll take a closer look at the demographic trends that irrefutably support our ever-growing Experience Economy and our vision for a new kind of CEO, the Chief Experience Officer. We will also explore why live events matter more than ever—for brands and for individual career trajectories.

CHAPTER 2

WHY LIVE?

Nothing happens without a live event.

–Scott Cullather

O ur prehistoric ancestors knew how to capture a live audience and use the visual power of the campfire, with its shadows and sparks, to tell stories that endure across millennia. During William Shakespeare's lifetime, the Bard employed elaborate stage devices to heighten his audience's experience: audio and visual effects, music, and even a theatrical cannon that misfired and sent the Globe Theatre up in flames in 1613. And when candidate John F. Kennedy faced down Richard Nixon on television as 40 percent of the nation's 180 million people tuned in,[9] presidential campaigns became a spectator sport overnight. "After that debate," explains Bruce DuMont, President of the Museum of Broadcast Communications and a nationally syndicated radio talk show host, "it was not just

---

9   Botelho, Greg. The Day Politics and TV Changed Forever. https://www.cnn.com/2016/02/29/politics/jfk-nixon-debate/index.html.

what you said in a campaign that was important, but how you looked saying it."[10] And yet, for too long corporate America seemed to have missed the memo. When investor or leadership meetings rolled out, all of the readily available energy and inspiration got stuck between floors. The result was a dreary, gray flannel aesthetic, in which all imaginative possibility had been reduced to didactic, show-off pieces. One old white guy after another (sorry, fellas!) espousing redundantly from the stage, reading off key metrics from an annual report, as their passive audience sat stiffly in their rental chairs, dreaming about lunch. A high point might be a gratuitous—and likely irrelevant—live entertainment interlude. Thank goodness we've emerged from those dark ages and are currently reconnecting to our essential storytelling natures.

Today, smart companies are using live events to position themselves as leaders in their respective spaces and across the global marketplace. Massive events like Salesforce's *Dreamforce* and the global TEDx franchise are influential thought leadership incubators. Even when their dimensions are more modest, live events give brands powerful opportunities to demonstrate transparency and collaboration, leveraging demographic trends to generate results. When 75 percent of millennials believe that attending a live event is more impactful than taking action online,[11] it's obvious where both the action and the marketplace are. There's simply nothing like live for gathering information, building strong constituencies, and creating a real sense of community alignment around core organizational identity and messaging. Live is the only barrier-free medium in the world that generates a direct and immediate connection to the attendee's heart, mind, body, and soul. With live, that fourth

---

10 Ibid.

11 Eventbrite, "The Experience Movement: Research Report,"accessed October 4, 2019, https://www.eventbrite.com/l/millennialsreport-2017/.

wall—the screen, the ad, the formerly closed system of an annual meeting—is removed. What emerges is a direct connection and a real conversation.

The combination of digital storytelling and live events may be our most powerful cultural symbiosis. Of course, social media amplifies live events, by extending their reach and impact. But social media can't exist without the content that live creates. Take a look at what's trending on Twitter or Instagram right now, and we bet you'll spot a live event behind it: live events create share-ability across social and digital channels. Conversely, digital and social provide live amplification and data capture. The combination of live and digital designed properly is not only popular but extremely potent. And yes, they generate earned media, far more valuable than paid media or traditional advertising.

Wielding their chosen social platforms, event attendees have emerged as citizen journalists. For millennials, attending a live event is far more than an activity—it's a form of self-expression,[12] where a communal gathering simultaneously becomes an individual's personal stage. When they actively engage with live and socialize about it afterward, their impact dwarfs that of an executive promoting their brand; this is how brands succeed today. Take this defining sensibility, then multiply it by the sheer force of population numbers, in which Generation Z now comprise 32 percent of the global population in 2019, nudging ahead of millennials,[13] and you get an absolutely platform-proof strategy. The apps may come and go, but live, as we've pointed out, has been around since the days of Adam and Eve.

---

12   Eventbrite, "The Experience Movement: Research Report,"accessed October 4, 2019, https://www.eventbrite.com/l/millennialsreport-2017/.

13   Miller, Lee J. and Wei Lu, *"Gen Z Is Set to Outnumber Millennials Within a Year"* https://www.bloomberg.com/news/articles/2018-08-20/gen-z-to-outnumber-millennials-within-a-year-demographic-trends.

OUR CLIENTS, OUR HEROES

Starting with the inception of INVNT, our goal was to create experiences rather than pedantic presentations. We pushed two of our very first clients to lean into their innate mastery of live and to permanently eschew podiums and speeches in favor of interactivity. And in turn, Fred DeLuca, co-founder and former CEO of Subway, and Indra Nooyi, former chairperson and CEO of PepsiCo, leveraged their powerful skills of the art form to exponentially grow their impressive careers to extraordinary heights. Fred taught us the power of Emotional Leadership. Indra taught us how to identify and harness the profound intersection of personal and public brand. In many ways, they are the parents of our proprietary live brand storytelling model.

FRED DELUCA: EMOTIONAL LEADERSHIP

Fred DeLuca, Co-founder and former CEO, Subway

It was the early '90s when Fred first keyed into the power of live—back when there were pay phones on every corner, we knew what busy signals and dialing up sounded like, and long before FaceTime. Fred's powerful presence at his franchisee conventions was a cornerstone of his leadership; he never missed a single one until, sadly, a leukemia diagnosis interfered.

Fred had a powerful tradition that became the high point of his annual conferences. Beaming out at his enormous constituency, Fred offered warm, enthusiastic words of welcome. He had everybody in the entire room stand up. He then invited all the first-time attendees to have a seat. Then he'd move on to anyone five years or less, then less than ten years, and so on, each time inviting those attendees to sit. Finally, only a handful of folks who'd been with the brand thirty or more years were left standing—his wife Liz, mom Carmela, sister Suzanne, and lifelong business partner Dr. Peter Buck. This masterful moment was the epitome of a global brand that was built on history, pride, motivation, and family values.

Fred's widow, Liz DeLuca, told us about the time that Fred prepared to share the next year's goal at the company annual meeting. "You're crazy," Liz remembered telling him. "We're never gonna hit that." But as Fred harnessed his audience of believers, and the live energy of the human connection electrified the room in real time, he emerged as a true emotional leader. The goal may have seemed outlandish, but gosh darn it, everyone was now going to strive to meet it. And they did.

Even as his business grew to a global powerhouse brand of over forty thousand restaurants in 110 countries, Fred remained a consistent and devoted presence.[14] He'd travel across the world to visit restaurants and meet with franchise owners, understanding that the live experience of being in the same room couldn't always be approximated by technology. These days it's become commonplace for companies to describe their culture as family. Fred's respect for

---

14   Subway, accessed October 8, 2019, https://www.subway.com/en-US/ ExploreOurWorld.

the power of live encouraged an emotional, connected culture, built the largest franchise chain in the history of quick-serve restaurants, and made him a franchise industry icon.

INDRA NOOYI:
EMBODYING THE BRAND

Indra Nooyi, Former Chairman and CEO, PepsiCo

Over the course of her twenty-four years with PepsiCo, Indra Nooyi used the mastery of the live event medium to define both her leadership style and her personal brand.

When Indra became President and CEO, she wanted to elevate her brand, especially in terms of her communication style with the top 250 people in her organization. Indra had been known for her formidable style, and she now wanted to take it to the next level. To get there, she was enthusiastic to break the mold. This wasn't going to be a dry presentation of the company's annual report; the goal was a performance energized with purpose and vision. Indra had to stand for PepsiCo's new direction—Performance With Purpose—that she, the first foreign born and female CEO in the history of PepsiCo, had set to define her vision for the global business.

Our event strategy began with the room. We installed a massive, floor to ceiling, curved projection wall. Standard issue event furniture was replaced with large, upholstered chairs grouped in the round and outfitted with push-to-talk microphones. Copies of Indra's recent

Fortune magazine cover story, ranking her as the number one most powerful woman in business, were placed on each seat. Her senior executives wouldn't just be comfortable; they'd be ridiculously comfortable. But luxurious individual seats had another meaning, too—they indicated autonomy and agency. These executives weren't going to be lined up like soldiers—they'd be comfortable and bolstered. And with microphones at their fingertips, they were in effect being invited to interrupt Indra, who wasn't there to hear the sound of her own voice, but to enrich her team's experience and empower them with ideas to develop their own leadership. This intention was underscored by an impressive roster of outside speakers, like the head of innovation at Google.

These methods worked so well that in 2010 Indra challenged us to push even further. When it was time to design her annual investor meeting, the team secured newly renovated Yankee Stadium, a Pepsi-pour venue. This giant arena had a personal connection to Indra, a rabidly passionate Yankees fan, and we made sure that every technological bell and whistle was employed to communicate Indra's openhearted embrace of her role as an extension of the brand. Looking back on her career, it's clear that the seeds of her extraordinary leadership legacy were planted during these defining live events.

STUDENTS OF LIVE: BREAKFAST, LUNCH, AND DINNER WITH SCOTT AND KRISTINA

Working with Fred, Indra, and so many of the other amazing leaders we have been blessed to call colleagues has been an incredible privilege and a lifetime learning experience that money can't buy. As we transitioned from employees to CEO and COO of our own agency, we applied their powerhouse examples as lessons in leadership. Above all else, Fred and Indra taught us that the value of connectivity at the heart of live belongs in the daily business of leadership. Indra didn't only hold court at Yankee Stadium; she regularly shared stories about her family life, letting her global team know that she called her mom every day, and suggesting they do the same. Fred never forgot that it was a thousand-dollar loan from his family friend, Dr. Peter Buck, that enabled him to open his first sandwich shop, and he always made sure his team was aware of his humble beginnings. These stories and more endeared—and connected—them as leaders.

Drawing from these lessons, we've established our own traditions. For example, we have established a monthly team meeting called *Breakfast, Lunch, and Dinner with Scott and Kristina*. We've identified the magical time of four o'clock in the afternoon, eastern standard time. Turns out, this is the only point on the dial when every one of our eight INVNT offices can chime in during waking hours. Our Sydney team is up early and having that first cup of coffee with us. INVNTrs in London are joining us for a glamorously late dinner. In San Francisco, the team is tucking in to lunch. And we're all together, connected both live and by video conference.

We pick a different topic for each meeting. We've gone through a list of what we call our "-isms": pithy phrases that express our values. We've led on leadership qualities we're striving to emulate. In the final fifteen minutes, we open up the floor, inviting our team to ask us anything they want: about the business, their careers, our lives. People actually go for it! We had a brand new, entry-level employee ask Scott what was up with his "Stay Weird" T-shirt. (Which Scott was rocking as part of his signature uniform: designer T-shirt, blazer, jeans, sneakers, and a crisp pocket square.) And we're asked difficult questions, too, like: "Is there a sector we wouldn't work with?" To that tough question, we had a tough tale, about a bid we walked away from for political and moral reasons. We've had our unlimited leave policy questioned. We'd installed the policy with the intention of attracting and sustaining high performers, but when a team member shared that he hadn't taken vacation in eighteen months, we had to re-evaluate how our bright ideas were actually functioning organizationally. *Breakfast, Lunch, and Dinner with Scott and Kristina* is a chance for us to personally connect, just like Fred showed us how. It's also a chance for us to design an event that embodies our personal brand, just as Indra taught us, reflecting the geographic range and diversity of our organization.

TAKEAWAY:
YOUR CAREER IS LIVE

Make each word tell.

– E. B. White

Live strategy isn't just essential to an organization's bottom line. The importance of skillful communication in a live format is arguably the single most important factor in a career trajectory, if not in human existence as a whole. A five-person meeting is a live event. A team meeting is a live event, too, as is a five thousand employee meeting. But the smaller the venue, the bigger the opportunity and, counterintuitively perhaps, the higher the stakes. For a general audience, a more general message can still be effective. But when it's you and four other people, every word counts. Posture counts. Facial expression counts. Vibration counts. Harnessing this power comes down to four key elements:

1. **GIVE 'EM THE CENTER CUT.** Craft the messaging around the selling points. Live demands focus: those are savvy, flesh and blood actual human beings in the audience, and they know when they're being sold to. So be concise and mindful of the true dimensions of the message.

2. **BE RESPECTFUL OF THEIR TIME.** Your audience is distracted—even as you're wowing them with a strategically crafted message, they're being bombarded by (literally) thousands of competing ones. Yours needs to be quick and to the point.

3. **KNOW YOUR AUDIENCE.** When engaging a seasoned, tenured audience, live event strategy

has got to pass the eye-roll test. What might land squarely on-target for a younger audience may be entirely off-key for the top eight hundred people at a *Fortune* 100 company. A senior team preparing a product launch at a big pharma company, let's say, has already been to a score of preparatory meetings; don't waste their time with what they already know (and it's your job to find out exactly what that is beforehand). Similarly, a CEO's leadership meeting has that executive's credibility on the line. In cases like these, achieving resonance is essential.

4. **THE F**K-IT FACTOR**. And yet ... perhaps as important as the eye-roll test, is the gut-check. Yes, we can slice it and dice it a hundred ways, or count on an algorithm, but sometimes with live, there's that "F**k-It Factor." As in, fuck it—I'm going with my gut and reaching for an ineffable, cosmic kind of fire that only I can see with my third eye.

WHAT'S NEXT

Coming up, we're doing the forensics of our "Challenge Everything™" battle cry. So much more than a tagline, this phrase is the philosophical cornerstone of all aspects of our business—it's our mantra and single guiding principle.

CHAPTER 3

CHALLENGE ƎVERYTHING

INVNT began during a time of grave economic turmoil that was somehow, simultaneously, a dazzling era for live events—with New York City as the crown jewel of the industry. There were so many juicy projects, so many major triumphs to read about in the papers, back when we all read newspapers. Standing in those early weeks and months of INVNT, however, we were feeling less sparkly and more jangled. Remember: Our brilliant career plan had exploded in our hands. We'd gotten pushed out in the middle of a recession. We were a little start-up officially headquartered in New York, staring up at a skyline of glittering Manhattan giants, wondering how we would ever convince anyone to hire us.

Right around then, we heard tell of an event produced by the sexiest agency of the moment that had scored the Rolling Stones as the headline act for a closing party, and were totally impressed while turning bright green with envy. (To this day, we're still unclear whether that tale is industry history or myth.) Scott would always open up *The New York Times*, read a few articles, and soon be shaking the business section in the air. "We should be doing this!" he'd exclaim frustratedly about the latest breakthrough event produced by a competitor. "Why aren't we doing this?"

"I don't know," Kristina would say, wanting to be a good partner while slowly being driven crazy. "You're the biz dev guy right? You go get it, and I'll produce the heck out of it."

And yet. That very same challenger mentality, the one that motivated us to pitch ourselves as capable successors to our former bosses, the one that had fired us up and then exploded—it emerged unscathed from the debacle. A challenger approach *still* felt right. It was *still* what we stood for, despite the setback we'd experienced. And so we clung to it, feeling deeply that it was the source of our strategy and that it would navigate us forward, despite being a scrappy start-up without the cred, or the financials, that the bigger companies did. We gathered up our grit and we kept going. And as those first years unfolded, we made "Challenge Everything" our official brand mantra. This wasn't copy, or color, or theater. "Challenge Everything" was, and still is, an apt expression of what we actually do and how we actually do everything. Not only how we develop breakthrough creative ideas, but how we engage with the marketplace, lead our organization and run it on the daily, and scout, recruit, and retain top talent.

THE CHALLENGER APPROACH: THE MARKETPLACE

We put our challenger concept to the test right away, by taking on the agency business model. We'd come up in a bricks and mortar culture: an equipment-heavy, asset-heavy, production-focused model. We stripped all that stuff away, emerging as—and remaining—a nimble model. Today, globally, we have one hundred–plus employees. "Holy crap," other agencies are likely to remark, "how are you going to accomplish two hundred projects with only one hundred or so employees?" Of course, these days our method is no longer uncommon, but back then, hiring only client-facing leads—the people that interact with the clients and sales—was unprecedented.

We began to build a lean, remarkable staff of creatives, including executive producers, designers, coordinators, and the like. We left the gear, the technical support teams, the audio engineers, all of that—on the cutting room floor. We told our clients: "We're not a traditional production company model. We're outsourcing all that stuff and we're going to be absolutely transparent about it: it's going to be a direct pass-through to you."

This tactic has given us long-term flexibility and growth, and allows us to deliver cost-effective, world-class service at the very best price. Managing global accounts from a central location, whether that's New York, London, or Sydney, and having offices in eight key cities, means that we can go anywhere in the world, travel from city to city, tap into our talented networks on the ground, and leverage our vendor networks to use the best technologies and platforms available. We're not hampered by the gear in which we've invested and that needs to generate a profit. Our solutions are designed by a small team of people who are carefully selected based on their skills, expertise, and suitability to the task at hand (which often means we'll have a truly global team working on any given project at any given time). They are responsible for making sure that the client relationship is airtight, and oversee all of the pieces. Production resources are curated locally—a move that also ensures our clients' experiences are tailored to and resonate with each unique audience group. We scale up and we scale down. It's a bespoke method. We're not forcing talent or technology on any projects. We're big, but we're not fat.

THE CHALLENGER APPROACH: PR + MARKETING STRATEGY

Since the beginning—and especially *at* the beginning—we've continued to spend approximately 8 percent of our operating budget on PR and marketing. Straight out of the gate, we knew that earned media would be a strategic cornerstone of our business development strategy, long before we had a fraction of the balance sheet we have today. We're of the belief that you can say all you want about your business, brand, work, and people, but it's the commentary from impartial, reputable third parties—the media—that carry more weight and get people to take notice (it's why we'll always advise our clients to ensure their live events are supplemented by a robust PR, as well as marketing strategy). This kind of coverage has incredible pull.

We see the value in awards, too. We are proud of our work, but to gain the recognition of others—that's powerful. Putting our very first shows up for awards enabled us to start gaining whatever earned media we could. Our wins quickly and effectively highlighted the quality of our work to clients and prospects in our creds decks and pitches.

By boldly telling a big story about our lean business even as our track record was still a work in progress, our Google footprint grew quickly; we passed our old agency on the left within the first six months.

And while our fledgling years may not have had the benefit of the Gram or Twitter, we're constantly evolving our approach. We've embraced these platforms with open arms (Scott's a bit of an influencer—and advocate—himself!), along with a slew of other digital marketing tools, to tell our story in an informative, editorially focused way. Our emphasis on media relations and earned media, though—that'll always remain.

THE CHALLENGER APPROACH: PHILANTHROPY

Our lean structure doesn't cramp our style when it comes to giving. We take a big boy, big corporate approach to philanthropy, making both cash and in-kind donations and giving approximately 5 percent of our EBITDA to charitable organizations. Doing this feels so good. But there's more to it: charitable giving is good for business, because it opens doors and meaningfully expands our network.

This commitment to giving also creates internal opportunities. We assign leadership roles for philanthropic projects to younger staffers to design and execute, allowing them to develop their chops and explore brilliant new ideas.

Recently, our talented associate producers led the 9th Annual Chris Carrino Foundation for FSHD Gala. Our friend Chris Carrino, a gifted sports journalist and broadcaster best known as the radio play-by-play voice of the Brooklyn Nets, is living with a type of muscular dystrophy known as facioscapulohumeral dystrophy, or FSHD, a genetic disorder that has resulted primarily in the progressive weakening of the muscles in his shoulders and upper limbs. In 2011 he established the Chris Carrino Foundation for FSHD, dedicated to improving the lives of those affected by facioscapulohumeral dystrophy. Held at Russo's on the Bay in the Howard Beach neighborhood of Queens, and typically hosting 800 people, this event raises much-needed funds for specifically focused scientific research.

Our super talented marketing intern designed and executed the social media campaign under the guidance of senior marketing and PR leadership. We also produced the live event, including visual identity design, script writing, audio and lighting design, and video production. Our coordinators designed and oversaw all elements of the auction event.

As a company, we show up. On any given weekend we gather as a group to support worthwhile causes by participating in awareness walks, softball games, golf tournaments, and the like. Recently, while on a work trip to DC, we met Kayla McKeon, the first Capitol Hill lobbyist with Down Syndrome, who invited us to get involved in a foundation with which she is affiliated, the National Down Syndrome Society (NDSS). Soon thereafter, a crowd of INVNTrs gathered in Central Park on a sunny Saturday to participate in the organization's New York City Buddy Walk—the local execution of a national initiative that sees three hundred thousand people participate in walks across the country. Needless to say, it was a great day.

Kristina drives the bulk of these initiatives, and Scott is actively involved in supporting them. A member of the First Responders Children's Foundation's (FRCF) board since 2015, he was named the organization's inaugural Corporate Hero in May 2019, in recognition of his ongoing support of the FRCF. This incredible organization provides much needed scholarships and financial aid to the children of fallen first responders.

THE CHALLENGER APPROACH: LEADERSHIP

We do more than challenge status quo processes: we challenge ourselves. We don't just come up with ideas, cross our fingers, and check back in two years later. We strive to be the first ones to own when an idea just isn't working. We're not afraid to look in the mirror and pivot: we're willing to fail fast when necessary.

Recently, we were developing an interactive learning/engagement event platform that we fully believed had promise. We even had a name for it that we liked: "Brew." As a board, we approved moving forward with the initiative, and we committed the necessary funds with the goal of a proof of concept at the three-month mark. When that proof of concept didn't deliver the results we had in mind, we killed the initiative, simple as that. We'll have learnings to apply to the next worthy idea, but in the meantime, we readily accept that all creative work typically involves a degree of attrition.

THE CHALLENGER APPROACH: HIRING

We don't want an overpopulated culture or layers of managers. We want the incredible talent we scout and hire to actually own their roles; this is why they have to be really good when we hire them. We are willing to take our time, willing to date before getting married. We consider it a mutual privilege and responsibility to be in business together, and so we're heavily curatorial.

Hire slow, fire smart: that's our hard-won motto when it comes to hiring. Our process is multidimensional, going far beyond mere HR vetting. A successful candidate is likely to have an incredible resume, but our close-knit culture is flesh and blood; candidates meet lots of people over the course of the interview process and must be a good fit temperamentally and energetically. We have seasoned INVNTrs take prospectives to lunch, while another group invites them to cocktails. It's a bit like rushing a coed fraternity. We ask our staff: Is this somebody they'd want to grab a bite with after work? How about a week spent on show site, with long hours, close quarters, and possibly very bad pizza? Would this person make a good dinner companion on the road?

We also encourage INVNTrs to help us shape the professional community we share with initiatives like Grand in the Hand. If any full-time employee recommends a hire that becomes a successful INVNTr, they get a thousand bucks for the referral.

And we are huge proponents of perma-lance. This became a practical tactic early on, but even today it's a valuable approach. When possible, unless we're poaching from another agency, we perma-lance for three to six months, in essence dating for a little while before committing. This works well for the potential employee, too, because we're not for everybody. For three to six months, we own their soul. They're a contracted employee with a formal restriction on freelancing for anyone else, and no benefits, yet. But that perma-lance window is enough time for us all to relax around one another and really get a sense of the fit. When it's time to decide if we're getting married, we've had enough time together—and enough bad pizza on the road—to be sure.

By now it's probably crystal clear: when it comes to hiring, we're not looking for warm bodies. We want people who are really, *really* good. And freelance creatives who are really good are really busy— we want them off the playing field. The story of our Chief Creative Officer, Paul Blurton, is a prime example. Paul's stellar reputation preceded him, which is how he landed on our radar in the first place. So of course, we wanted to book him for every RFP that rolled in. Except we'd reach out, and he'd be booked. As in, every single freakin' time. Finally, we implored him: "Dude! When are you not booked?"

There was a beat as Paul consulted his calendar. "I free up in January of next year," he began to calculate …

We pounced. "Great! We'll take you from January to June."

Paul looked a little uncertain, as you can well imagine. "What am I working on?" he inquired.

"We don't know," we replied. What we *did* know was that Paul was worth both the risk and the investment. After all, Paul's six-month fee at his then A-lister day rate was going to be a major line item for our budget year. Paul promised to think about it, and later, over a drink, we started processing the sticker shock. "What the hell is he going to work on?" Kristina asked.

"It doesn't matter," Scott replied. "We secured the talent. And when the word gets out that we got Paul Blurton, the business is gonna roll right in on that wave."

And guess what—Scott was right.

Paul gave us six months. "Just so you know," he said as we were synching our calendars, "I'm happy to freelance with you ... but I'm never going full-time. Never."

"Of course," we told him. "We get it."

Time passed, the creative chemistry was undeniable, and soon it was clear Paul was entertaining a change in status. "Just promise me that we are not going to settle for the ordinary and that we will develop a plan to really shake this industry up and do creative and strategic work that has never been done," he demanded, good-naturedly.

"We will," we told him. "We do festivals. We open luxury hotels across the International Date Line." Cut to: Not only did Paul come on board, but eleven years later he's a major shareholder and leads the creative team that he built for our entire operation.

What caused Paul's shift in mission statement? It helped that we offered him his own department, with the chance to build his own team and train them the way he wanted to. In short, we were offering Paul carte blanche to develop his vision, with the creative bandwidth to go a little crazy. Soon, the best creatives in the business flocked to INVNT to be on Paul's team. And it certainly helped that we offered attractive benefits with three different health plans, one of which pays 100 percent of an employee's insurance (as we'd done from day one).

And from there, from that calculated risk, the fees started flowing in, because we were winning everything.

Today, we open the trades (reading them on our phones on the go) and, seeing the giant Samsung launch or the impressive Genesis reveal, we say: "Hey! Why didn't we … oh. Wait a second, we *did* do that!" And as many times as we've had the opportunity to make that exact same joke, we still get how amazing it is, and we're still humbled and incredibly proud to be standing in the reality that was once the dream.

TAKEAWAYS:

SIGNS IT'S A CHALLENGER CONCEPT. The idea floats up in a brainstorm, or wakes you up in the middle of the night, and it's like an insistent tap from the inside. In fact, it freaks you out: when you imagine pitching this idea to the client, you have no idea how it might go, but man are you psyched to give it a shot. The hair on the back of your neck stands on end and maybe there's some queasiness. All signs point to Challenger!

ASK YOURSELF WHAT YOU DON'T NEED. Take the time to examine every process and procedure for its company-wide impact. Clarity about what the business *doesn't* need, and a subsequent jettisoning of obsolete processes, are without doubt as powerful as initiating a project, initiative, or direction.

THE POWER SEAT IS NUMBER TWO. There's no brand that shouldn't be a challenger: our economy is littered with felled giants, once-dominant companies like Howard Johnson's or Blockbuster whose complacency led to their untimely demise. Being number two has enormous benefits, because it generates drive, determination, enthusiasm, and the collective energy needed to engineer brilliant creative risk. In our experience, number two status is nothing short of propulsive.

WHAT'S NEXT

Coming up, we're taking a closer look at both the structure and engineering of our business, and our approach to attracting, retaining, and managing our stellar creative talent.

CHAPTER 4

SECRET SAUCE: THE TRIBE

> *You need to put on a pair of shoes a few sizes too big, and grow into them.*
>
> **–Scott Cullather**

EMOTIONAL LEADERSHIP

What a gift to have witnessed the power and possibility of emotional leadership up close, in the course of our collaborations with Fred DeLuca, Indra Nooyi, and dozens of other extraordinary leaders: these lessons were crucial as we started INVNT. We knew we'd be going up against the big boys, and that to win we'd need to change the game. Everything about our brand would have to look, feel, smell, and taste entirely new: not just a departure from the status quo, but from who we'd been in our (not so distant) past lives. Given that Scott's dad began his career with Jack Morton, it was a coincidence of mythic proportions that *Fortune* magazine recognized us in their *David vs. Goliath* column for "going head to head with more established rivals during a recession," and specifically for facing down Jack Morton.[15] Reinvention was agenda item one. "Scalable and sustainable" became our key operating principle.

David vs. Goliath

inVNT vs. Jack Morton Worldwide

2 of 3 « BACK | NEXT »

The challenge: Going head-to-head with more established rivals -- during a recession!

What they did: Launching a liveevents agency during the 2008 slump was kind of risky. But with 21 years in the industry, Scott Cullather was certain the market would welcome a lean, independent startup as an alternative to firms like the giant Interpublic Group's Jack Morton. He and his four partners, based in New York and Washington, D.C., tapped their network to sign corporate accounts like PepsiCo and associations such as the Society of Human Resource Management.

One key strategy: helping clients quantify the impact of meetings by tracking things like social-media mentions using new analytics tools. For big events, the firm relies on a group of experienced freelancers and contractors. Sales were $19.2 million in 2010, up 101% over the prior year -- and inVNT says it was profitable.

NEXT: Arkay Packaging vs. International Paper

BY ELAINE POFELDT - LAST UPDATED FEBRUARY 01 2012: 12:30 PM ET

*There's nothing more powerful than
earned media, especially early on.*

We knew that our new venture would need to embody a vision that came *from* us, but that would ultimately transcend us. What we'd seen at our former agency, as well as among competitors, was the downside of hanging out a shingle emblazoned with a single name. Sure, there was an initial rush of ego-fueled adrenaline—a fantastic (and fleeting) hit of ownership and, quite literally, of agency. But this strategy, time and time again, created the expectation for clients that it will be "you or nothing," at all times, for all reasons. This narrow channel can restrict growth, for the business as a whole and individual

---

15   Pofeldt, Elaine. "David vs. Goliath," *Fortune*, February 1, 2012.

team members, too: instead of hanging up a shingle, we put on a pair of shoes five times too big. In doing so, we forced ourselves to look at where we were going and how to get there. What emerged from that initial strategy was an intentional culture, designed to require more than just the two of us. We wanted to attract the best and the brightest, and so we made room for them. In fact, the idea from the beginning was to, one day, make ourselves obsolete.

Our vision, "to be The Global Live Brand Storytelling Agency," inextricably linked to our "challenge everything" mantra, is put to the test on the daily now that we've grown many times in size. We remain firm believers that when you challenge the status quo the most disruptive and striking ideas emerge, and that this core value is scalable to our ongoing expansion. We don't want to wake up one morning to find we've become a version of the Goliaths we once defied. With every choice we make, from office layouts designed to mitigate hierarchy and generous employee incentives to our personal presence at pitches all over the world, we recommit to remaining a Big Small Agency. This concept was introduced to us by John Wringe, our Nonexec Chairman, whom we affectionately refer to as "Uncle John." The Big Small Agency ethos is based on welcoming and encouraging expansion, pride in limitless creative power, but never losing sight of our core values. We show up for tasks that senior executives regularly farm out or phone in—joyful ones like attending our team members' weddings and baby showers, and tough ones, like personally flying halfway around the world to let an employee go. We demand accountability from our teams and from ourselves.

Which is how Scott emerged as our Process Prophet.

Every business needs a process prophet.

Process is easily feared. Too much strangles an enterprise. Not enough, those good ideas can spoil as the whole endeavor spins out of control. What's emerged for us over time, trial, and error are Eight Principles of Leadership. They reflect INVNT's core organizational values, which in turn inform our process.

LEADERSHIP PRINCIPLE 1 | BE A CHALLENGER.

No matter how big or successful an enterprise becomes, it's essential to maintain a start-up consciousness—or, even better, an underdog consciousness. The bigger a venture gets, the less relevant risk-taking may seem. But safety is the best friend of failure, because it breeds mediocrity. Maintaining a challenger mind-set is absolutely essential to the INVNT brand because it keeps us out of the safe lane, energizes our long-standing client relationships, and is often a straight shot to success in the marketplace: we regularly win business from incumbent agencies who've become complacent. With offices in eight cities in five countries on four continents, we have teams living and working in different societies, different time zones. We celebrate those differences, and at the same time, when recruiting staff, we seek a certain kind of bold attitude that combines a disciplined, self-directed vision with the drive to take convention-busting, blow-shit-up risks. This challenger mind-set is more than a desirable trait—it both defines and unites our brand and our tribe.

LEADERSHIP PRINCIPLE 2 | BE CULTURE CRAZY.

The north star of our high performance, high growth organization is our culture. Every time our INVNTrs (our affectionate shorthand for our people) get comfortable, we ask them to readjust as we grow. The fact is, whether we're on the road or prepping a pitch, the hours are long, and the work is intensely collaborative. Our culture fuels our success because it generates the energy and support—that going of the extra mile—talented and creative people need to do their best work. We make an additional and significant fiscal investment in this value by bringing our entire company together for a tribe-wide meeting. Once a year, for three days, we're face to face for evaluation, celebration, and motivation. Given the sincere and mutual investment we're all making and the equity we share, this event feels like a homecoming.

LEADERSHIP PRINCIPLE 3 | FOCUS ON GREAT.

Our vision, to be the global live brand storytelling agency, naturally requires growth. How do we protect the precious resource of our brand DNA while scaling at an impressive pace? By applying this principle to our philosophy of scale.

During a recent company growth spurt, we heard grumblings to the tune of: "Oh my God, we're understaffed." We were interviewing, but our people were frustrated. On one of our quarterly, tribe-wide calls, Kristina said to take a look around at our incredible level of talent. "Please, please know we don't want you guys to suck it up and work harder," Kristina implored, naming some of our most respected team members, "It's hard to find more of you!" This was an honest plea, and may have earned us a smidge of forgiveness and extra time as we mindfully grew our team. In the beginning, we may have hired anyone literate with a pulse. But today, we focus on great. That means holding out for quality and holding on to our values, even under pressure.

LEADERSHIP PRINCIPLE 4 | WORK ON THE BUSINESS VS. IN THE BUSINESS. "On the business" and "in the business": These are the two interconnected pillars of daily focus and effort that support the INVNT vision. When we're working "OTB," we're thinking about our brand, our trajectory, our EBITDA, and our growth: looking out, not down. We do this by embracing what we call "The Five Ds":

- **DISCOVER.** The same line of clear-eyed inquiry we pursue in assessing a client's goals applies to the continued development of our own business. Regardless of the objective, a discovery process is just as powerful a tool for daily tasks. Thoughtful consideration of "What are my tasks today and what do we need to accomplish them?" is an effective counterpoint to reactivity, and the inefficiency that tends to result.

- **DEFINE.** Clarity is a key component of success, and it's always the result of the discovery process. You'll hear us say this again and again, because it's absolutely fundamental: If you don't know where you're headed, how can you get there?

- **DEVELOP.** Here's where we construct the road map. Starting with the goal in mind, we work backwards to engineer a plan of action.

- **DELIVER.** Aaaaand—GO! The execution phase, fueled by the preceding steps, often seems to flow naturally. That's the beauty of a well-constructed plan.

- **DEBRIEF.** We don't just hurtle forward to the next task— we take the time to reflect on what went well and what can be improved for next time.

Working on the business means that we put operational savvy ahead of the status quo. Here's a motto we love to hate: "If it's not broke, don't fix it." *So* not how we do things: we are constantly, relentlessly evaluating our business, combing through all aspects of the organization in search of refinements.

Kristina looked around one day and challenged our internal telecom setup. "Our entire business design is based on an open floor plan," she observed, "so why do we have a phone plan based on office phones? Nobody's using them—we're all on our cell phones." So we got rid of our phone system, kept the main line for each office, and installed a new, streamlined system, and saved eighty grand that we would much rather spend on business development or operational improvements.

We were also early adopters of the movement away from production books. Any show changes a thousand times from the moment the deal closes to the moment the curtain closes. We train our producers to run their shows based off their laptop and two pieces of paper. We're not about felling a forest of trees every time we load in a show.

When we're in "ITB" mode, we're focused on project management, deliverables, client relationships, and business development. As partners in business and in life, we're always balancing (and rebalancing) our distinct spheres of influence with our intention to lead cohesively and harmoniously. Today, Kristina has close to a fifty-fifty balance. Half of her time is focused on day-to-day operations ("in the business"), with the other half forecasting the future ("on the business"). Scott's primary role is working on the business: he spends 95 percent of his time looking out and not down.

One of our most essential INVNT "OTB" pillars is a single profit and loss statement across all our different offices. While our eight offices function interdependently, compensation, bonuses, time accrual, and expenses ladder up into one cohesive portrait of our unified performance. Structuring our business with a global mind set prevents our teams from facing one another in competition, and bases bonus compensation on the holistic profitability of the agency: a win in one region is celebrated and rewarded company-wide. Plus, it means we're able to curate project teams based on expertise rather than location, ensuring our clients receive the highest quality work possible.

LEADERSHIP PRINCIPLE 5 | GIVE 'EM SKIN IN THE GAME. Leadership equity grants may be the single most powerful move we've made, and it's come from the most painful lessons we've learned. We know all too well how it feels, and how things can go, when an agency treats its talent like renters instead of owners.

Giving our leaders financial ownership through stock is half of it—almost a third of our top INVNTrs have stock in the company, and at our recent company annual meeting we announced a widening of that pool. The other half is sharing brand ownership by encouraging decision-making authority. Real autonomy is critical for attracting high-performing people and maintaining their commitment and involvement.

LEADERSHIP PRINCIPLE 6 | PLAN AND FORECAST.

The big agency we came from may have planned and forecasted, but nothing was shared. That's one of the practices we blew up. Today, we plan and forecast well in advance of the following fiscal year and share our intentions openly, along with regular updates throughout the year, during our quarterly tribe wide calls and aforementioned breakfast/lunch/dinner meetings. In our company, across all eight offices, everyone knows exactly where we are at the end of each quarter.

We ensure our people know how their own performance is evolving, too. Our feedback culture encourages regular, honest, open conversation that's not tied exclusively to a formal review structure. Our internal "Cammies" awards, bestowed at our Company-wide Annual Meeting (CAM), recognize MVPs across departments, while the Grand Cammy is given to the INVNTr of the year, and INVNTr of the Month initiatives recognize and reward performance. (Plus there are annual reviews, too!) All of this insight informs the management of individual projects and empowers our leadership to strategically determine the bets we want to put on the table and those to pass on.

LEADERSHIP PRINCIPLE 7 | CREATE A SCALABLE, SUSTAINABLE BUSINESS MODEL.

When we first started INVNT and our staff could be counted on one hand, every day was an annual meeting. In a constant mode of improvisation, we were evolving on the fly. As we began to grow, and our head count expanded to about twenty-five people, we held a formal annual meeting to focus on our collective vision. The theme: *Growing Up*. We had fun with it, and everybody shared kid photos of themselves. But we were also at a critical juncture. Unchecked growth, we knew, could have disastrous consequences. To do it right, we'd need to harness that initial surge of growth to build a business model we could sustain over time.

We'd gone from ten to twenty million in one year, and it was clearly time to stop running and gunning. We didn't want to reconsider our model. But when we looked in the mirror, what we saw bore an eerie resemblance to the famous Lucille Ball bit with the candy factory conveyor belt (see image): we had to fix a few things. To create and manage a scalable, sustainable business plan we began with defining

our culture, setting the bar for our staff, and slowing the hiring process way down. It was right at this moment that our accountant informed us we'd outgrown him. Eventually we found a brilliant and principled CFO in Wolf Karbe, who is also a board member, to helm a dedicated finance team.

LEADERSHIP PRINCIPLE 8 | KEEP YOUR DOORS OPEN 24/7. Quality of life is important to us, and we continue to design guardrails to protect our team members from burning out. One general rule is that we "respect the weekend" when possible. From Friday evening to Monday morning, INVNTrs who happen to be working avoid inundating colleagues with emails, unless they're time sensitive. That being said, "doors open" means we're available and accessible as leaders of our business, and in service to our global clients, on a "world clock" schedule; with offices in multiple time zones, the lights are always on. For example, Thanksgiving is a holiday

only celebrated by Americans. So, guess what's likely to happen on Thanksgiving Day? Our international clients are working, our vendors are working, our business partners are working—and that means we're working. "Work/life balance" is a popular phrase, but our business model more closely resembles an infinity loop of work/play/work/play. For us, the phrase "work/life blend" is a better descriptor of INVNT culture; it's an infinity cycle whereby we never really come in and out of work, we're never really off the grid, and in doing so we're able to find a proper blend that enables us to continue to grow, but at the same time prevents us from burning out.

CULTURE + TALENT

Our process isn't separate from our culture. It's the stabilizing container that holds our cultural values, and that sustains the quality of creative energy and purpose that defined the very earliest days of our agency. And process without talent is just an empty loft space. And so, we hire people who embody our prin-

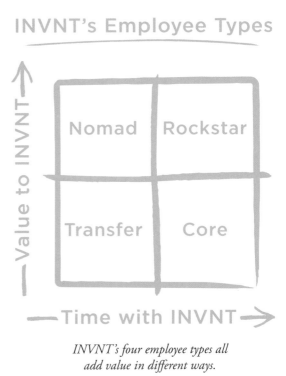

INVNT's four employee types all add value in different ways.

ciples—who, even after their best day at work, ask: "What's next?" We've come to call them "wicked smart teenagers." This designation has nothing to do with chronological age and everything to do with attitude, beliefs, and values.

The INVNT mind set requires voraciousness for learning, passion for the work, risk-seeking, and zero tolerance for average. There's also rebelliousness, a degree of hubris, and sense of invincibility in the mix. That makes for a healthy representation of rock stars across our agency: big personalities with extreme levels of creative output and stamina who bring in business and thrive in the resulting spotlight. But no agency wants to be staffed with 100 percent rock stars. That's why core employees are essential: their contributions reflect steadiness, high levels of competency, and commitment. Nomads contribute impressively, but their personal trajectory is their priority; they come in the door already engineering their next move. New team members are a question mark. We know they'll evolve, and we spend the first three months of their tenure becoming clearer not just on whether they'll work out, but what trajectory they're most likely to follow.

We use this profiling methodology not to limit or categorize our team members, nor to put anyone in a box, but as a leadership tool that helps us wisely and accurately decide how we want to invest in our team. Typically, our most successful employee investments have occupied the right side of the quadrant, in a split between core and rock star.

We want our core employees to know their value, and that their day in, day out contributions are essential to our navigating the balance of scale and sustainability.

We want to convert nomads into rock stars, giving them a reason to stay (and discouraging them from moving on with our IP in tow). That being said, some nomads are simply built to be rolling stones. It's not always realistic to change their creative or personal natures.

In those cases, it's valuable to leverage their contributions while we have them.

We've also learned over time that our culture does not respond well to hasty promotions, and that the threat of quitting is never a reason to promote. We expect and demand great things of each other, but most importantly ourselves. Promoting someone too early sets them up for failure, sets the clients/customers up for disappointment, and leads our tribe to rightfully ask us: "What on earth were you thinking?" (Not something we want to see in the mirror!)

The industry grapevine has served our recruitment process many times. We know what we're looking for and we know when we've found it. We're particularly focused on handpicking the leadership we install to helm our offices. Before Jerry Deeney, who runs our Detroit office and sits on our board of directors, joined our team, he was our competitor. Jerry was introduced to us by a client, after he called on her and she was suitably impressed, but explained she was committed to her partnership with us. So, Jerry reached out (baller move!) and met with Scott during an airport layover. Their creative chemistry was so immediate and energized that they both missed their flights.

We let recruits know they can write their own script with us. This isn't altruism—it's entrepreneurialism at its best. We'll say it again: in order to build a scalable, sustainable

Kristina is passionate about nurturing the next generation of talent.

business, we need to attract and retain high performing people, and those people must be allowed to chart their destinies. Individual ownership is the basic human right that's helped one of our rock star designers who joined us as a freelancer in New York, grow into launching and running our SWDSH Design Studio in Stockholm, and other INVNTrs navigate from operations to creative, production to biz dev, or from one country to another.

From day one, Kristina has always emphasized the importance of mentoring: it effectively equips our teams with the tools they need to develop and the inspiration required to create and uphold our leadership position in the industry. What we've observed is that the desire to continuously improve is largely universal, and that drive, motivation, and passion are leading traits among INVNTrs. Mentoring is so much more than a professional favor or an act of altruism: it's a canny investment in the future of our enterprise. (And it feels great to pass along experience and wisdom to younger colleagues who appreciate them!)

FIVE MENTORSHIP ESSENTIALS

MENTORSHIP ESSENTIAL 1 | SHARE YOUR STORIES.

Rather than take the textbook approach and recall a generic "what if" situation, share personal anecdotal experiences with your mentees. These real-life reflections will be more relatable, and they'll allow your team to visualize how they might apply your strategies in similar situations. This act of connectivity is also humanizing—embracing this dimension would benefit many leaders.

MENTORSHIP ESSENTIAL 2 | LOOK BEYOND THE BOARDROOM.

While a career mentor is important, encourage your mentees to develop a team of mentors who represent a range of contexts and attributes.

Kristina considers herself fortunate to have found mentors from across her diverse network of associates, among her intersecting social, client, vendor, and family circles. Mentors can come from anywhere as long as you keep your eyes and ears open for them. When you do find someone who will take the time to mentor you in an area where you seek personal improvement, do not pass that opportunity up.

MENTORSHIP ESSENTIAL 3 | READ, READ, READ ... THEN LISTEN.

With so much knowledge at our fingertips courtesy of the Information Age, we encourage mentees to seek out books and podcasts from successful marketing professionals and entrepreneurs. These resources offer a break from the day-to-day of "working in the business" and deliver "working on the business" inspiration. One of Kristina's personal faves: *Powerful: Building a Culture of Freedom and Responsibility*, by Patty McCord of Netflix.

MENTORSHIP ESSENTIAL 4 | GIVE REVERSE MENTORSHIP A TRY.

When mentorship is treated as a two-way street, its benefits multiply. Want to increase your social media savviness? Take a Gen Zer out to lunch and have them share their tips on photographing and hashtagging an experience so that it generates more engagement on social media—assuming the role of student could get your post trending!

MENTORSHIP ESSENTIAL 5 | FOSTER AND COMMUNICATE AN OPEN-DOOR POLICY.

Don't just keep the door open—actively demonstrate your advocacy for this approach. Encourage your team to seek you out for insight and advice, and remind them that while a mentoring relationship can develop organically, sometimes they need to articulate a request for support and involvement. Being present as a leader supports a transparent culture where feedback can flow regularly and comfortably, beyond a formal annual review structure. When leaders and teams develop a mutually supportive understanding of career goals and trajectories, they can be incredibly effective joining forces on the path to getting there.

Of course, from time to time, we part ways with team members. Sometimes people move on, sometimes we get disappointed, and sometimes we do the disappointing: that's life. Yes, we identify as emotional leaders—but stable leaders detach their emotions from their decisions. There's no value in getting dramatic about individual personnel changes, even when they sting. The job demands that we make the tough calls, communicate respectfully, treat transitions transactionally, and move on. We're personally responsible for the well-being of the agency and by extension for the individuals—and their families—that are entrusted to us as employers. Of course, we have enormous emotion regarding our business, but we're investing it in the holistic whole.

TAKEAWAYS: BEINGS, NOT DOINGS

1. **INVEST IN YOUR MOST IMPORTANT ASSETS.** In our case it's our tribe—the actual human beings whose brilliance and hard work fuels the INVNT universe. And we'd venture that in your endeavors it's also the imaginative minds and diligent contributors that are determining, on a daily basis, the likelihood of your vision becoming a reality. Simply put, take good care of your people and remember that their experience has a direct relationship to your success.

2. **BE A SERVANT LEADER, NOT A DICTATOR.** Ask yourself on both a daily and task by task basis: "How can I be of service?" This is an entirely different paradigm from "What will it take to win?"—and yet, it proves itself, time and time again, to be an enormously powerful engine of success, goodwill, and a healthy professional culture.

3. **ALWAYS PUT THE GOOD OF THE WHOLE AHEAD OF THE INDIVIDUAL—EVEN IF IT APPLIES TO YOU.** The first part may seem like a no-brainer: in any group situation, the enterprise must be understood as a living, breathing organism, and its health requires a holistic view. The second part is harder. As leaders, our job is to steward the big picture, and sometimes that means our own preferences get the high hard one. We usually live to tell the tale!

4. **MENTOR AT LEAST ONE PERSON IN YOUR LIFETIME.** It will be the most rewarding thing you do.

PART TWO

THE
WORK

CHAPTER 5

FROM CHAOS TO CLARITY: THE 7 STEPS OF INVNTion™

> Yesterday's "Wow!" is tomorrow's "So what?"
>
> **–Paul Blurton,**
>
> Chief Creative Officer, INVNT
> (without whom this chapter would not exist)

INVNTion™ takes clients from chaos to clarity.

Whether we're developing a brand-new campaign or working with a return client, our proprietary methodology takes clients from chaos to clarity: what emerges on the other side is a meaningful live brand storytelling game plan.

We call this consistent, flexible process "the journey from red to green—INVNTion™." Its seven steps are tried and true. What begins as a complex tangle of strategies, messages, objectives, brand/product information, and ideas—lots of them!—spanning different stakeholders is carefully unraveled. Our role is to tease out patterns and insights, applying clarity and focus so that a strong and actionable concept can emerge. By the time the brand is in the spotlight, the message is clear, consistent, and precise. Maybe in the GPS age it's old school to value a road map. But this one has never let us down.

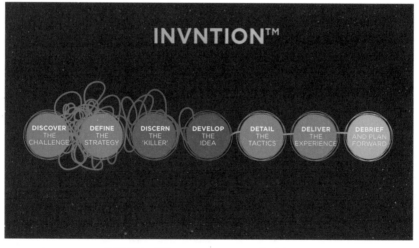

INVNTion's™ seven steps are tried and true.

STEP 1 | DISCOVER THE CHALLENGE.

This is the cornerstone—the foundation. Without a properly conducted discovery phase, what could be an exquisitely engineered campaign could better resemble a "house of cards."

That being said, the discovery phase is a tender time in the life of a client relationship and a project: it requires delicacy and diplomacy. Our discovery process begins with a bunch of questions. We give our clients the heads up that what may sound purely philosophical will in fact be immensely valuable to us, and to them. We want our questions to be understood as a method of achieving insight, not a stressful interrogation (or worse, an indication that we have doubts about their competence).

The essential question is "Why?" As in: "Why are you investing in this initiative?" What we are aiming for is the "core need"—something we can actually influence and change. Usually, it takes about five rounds of questioning to arrive at the core reason. This exploration tends to go something like this:

ROUND 1 INVNT: "Why are you going in this direction?"

CLIENT: "Because we always do this."

ROUND 2 INVNT: "Well … why do you always do this?"

CLIENT: "Because it's an integral part of the sales organization."

ROUND 3 INVNT: "Why is it an integral part of the sales organization?"

CLIENT: "Because it improves our revenue stream."

ROUND 4 INVNT: "And why does it improve your revenue stream?"

You get the point, right? But wait, there's more. Because at round five, we get to the gold.

ROUND 5 INVNT: "And why does it improve your revenue stream?"

Wait for it …

> **CLIENT:** *"Because our sales teams leave the meeting super motivated."*

Aha! *Now* we've arrived at the core need, which helps inform our objectives and leads to the next step of defining the strategy. Because now we know that the central criteria of the event is to motivate the sales team. We can't walk into a meeting and say: "we're here to increase revenue"—that's truly not in our hands, and it would be a foolish thing to promise. To motivate their sales people, however— now *that* we can do exceptionally well.

With the core need in hand, we'll move on to more practical questions to help us gain clarity on the scope of the live experience itself. We want to understand our client's intentions and expectations around head count, demographic profile of attendees, venue dates, and budget. Are there other key deliverables down the road? Does the event goal include measurement or social strategy?

DISCOVER THE CHALLENGE | GENESIS MINT CONCEPT LAUNCH

BEST PRACTICE | THERE'S NO SUCH THING AS TMI: IMMERSE YOURSELF.

The Genesis Mint Concept Launch was the first official event to be held at New York's Hudson Yards.

For the Genesis Mint Concept launch, we had two brand new partners, Genesis and their creative agency, INNOCEAN USA. We also had a new venue, Hudson Yards in New York City, the home of the now world-famous Vessel, which hadn't yet housed a major event like the one we'd been tasked to create. This was a notable pile-up of high-stakes firsts to be unpacked, examined, reviewed, and coordinated.

Our core task was helping Genesis unveil its new vehicle in front of both a live audience of media and VIP influencers, and a virtual one of millions of curious consumers. The experience needed to highlight the Mint Concept's luxury lifestyle and design-led thinking, while serving a robust content strategy—made possible by our story studio, HEVĒ (and there'll be more on HEVĒ in the next chapter).

We didn't just have to arrive at mastery of voice, personalities, and parameters. We had to blend the goals and objectives of two teams, and develop and nurture new and productive relationships. We needed to make sure that our event design both honored and protected the remarkable space that would house it. And so, we used every bit of our three-month runway prelaunch to become totally immersed, helping ourselves to just as many questions as we needed to ask—which, it turns out, were countless.

RESULT HIGHLIGHTS | The event was filled to capacity, attracting 250+ journalists and VIP guests—well above the brand's target. Twitter livestream views topped 450,000, and a branded content campaign running across a series of Condé Nast's most renowned titles saw four million impressions in its first two days alone. Seventy-five media outlets covered the launch: *The New York Times* called it "one of the hottest tickets in town,"[16] and the team at *Architectural Digest* described it as a "festive event [that] had all the makings for a company that was intent on making a statement to consumers—and competitors".[17] An INVNT-distributed press release reached 10.2 million readers within less than a week of the event date, delivering even greater cut-through for the new vehicle.

STEP 2 | DEFINE THE STRATEGY.

The strategy is not the idea. The strategy is not the tactical pull-through, or the package, or the campaign. *The strategy is the vision that we'll follow.* It's built from what we heard—our under-

---

16   Tom Voelk, "Before New York Auto Show, Cars Take Their Own Star Turns," *The New York Times*, April 17, 2019, https://www.nytimes.com/2019/04/17/business/2019-new-york-auto-show-events.html.

17   Nick Mafi, "Genesis Unveils Its Mint Concept Car in New York's Hudson Yards," *Architectural Digest*, April 17, 2019, https://www.architecturaldigest.com/story/genesis-unveils-mint-concept-car-new-york-hudson-yards.

standing of a brand's pillars. Sometimes these elements are explicitly communicated by a brand in the discovery meeting, but often we're helping our clients articulate the strategic pillars that will eventually ladder down to the tactics. The INVNT approach is always on brand, on point, on message—but disruptive. We combine our values with our clients', and this brew is distilled into the strategy that guides how we're going to approach both the business as a whole and creative development, specifically.

This insight is recorded in *The Comms Brief*, an essential tool in the definition of strategy and the guide to everything else that follows. This is a practical document that's not trying to be colorful—it's got a serious job to do, which is to unite INVNT's insights with a brand's strategy, messaging, and explicit communication goals and objectives. It translates those ideas into a set of guiding principles and big ideas that will inform creative development. Constructed in open dialogue with clients and key stakeholders, *The Comms Brief* becomes the collective handshake that defines our shared intention and game plan. Time and again, having our mutual coordinates set and confirmed via *The Comms Brief* results in fewer creative and strategic cul-de-sacs, while setting a barometer to evaluate potential changes in direction as they inevitably arise. Bottom line: It's hard to stay on the same page if you don't have a page.

DEFINE THE STRATEGY | XEROCON | "MAKE ACCOUNTING COOL"

BEST PRACTICE | WHEN THEY ZIG ... WE ZAG.

Xerocon has a reputation for being the "Coachella for Accountants."

The global small business platform Xero operates in a crowded market, and the brand subsequently wanted to offer its audiences something different from—and much more memorable than—its competitors' efforts. With a portfolio of products designed and produced for businesses with one hundred employees or fewer, the brand's intention wasn't to compete with enterprise software programs. So, we zigged away from a comparison story and zagged our way to: "Make accounting cool."

The colorful, energized, heart-pounding Xerocon event we created in collaboration with our bold Xero clients is now referred to as the "Coachella for Accountants," a term coined by the media. Xerocon attendees truly look forward to meaningful educational content brimming with exciting activations and networking activities: a perfect balance of fun, play, and information.

RESULT HIGHLIGHTS | With 3,300-plus attendees, and named by the A-List Guide as Australia's best event of the year,[18] Xerocon enjoyed extensive press coverage across industry and mainstream media including *Sky News*, *Forbes*, *The Australian Financial Review*, and *Campaign*. The #Xerocon hashtag trended on Twitter and saw 6,300 mentions and 30,300 engagements on social media, and it won awards across all corners of the globe. Having grown the account from local to global, INVNT and Xero teams now collaborate across multiple geos.

STEP 3 | DISCERN THE 'KILLER.' This concept is one of our key differentiators. The Killer is the north star of a campaign: not the idea, not the campaign, not the theme. It's a single word or short phrase that we establish at the top of the process, and it guides us as we develop the idea and travel through the subsequent steps.

Once we share the Killer with our client and achieve consensus, we have the ultimate compass—a single, unifying thought—to keep us on track at every stage of the development process. If what we're doing deviates from the Killer, we pause to reflect, ask ourselves if what we're doing is right, and consider our options. Should we change the Killer? Should we reshape our thinking to course correct back to the Killer?

---

18   "A LIST Guide's Top 5 Events of 2018," December 12, 2018, https://alistguide.com.au/blog/top-5-events-of-2018/.

DISCERN THE 'KILLER' | MIELE | "ARTISTRY"

BEST PRACTICE | CONNECT THE DOTS TO THE BRAND'S SELF-IMAGE.

The Miele experience more than paid for itself in forty-eight hours.

Miele was rightfully proud of the beauty of its new washer/dryer interiors, and wanted to share the product design's overall combination of precision, technology, high design, and efficiency with the press and consumers. What we saw was a work of museum-worthy art. "Artistry" became the Killer for this project, a through line that traveled from the brand's self-image to every single beat of a unique theatrical experience held in London, in which light, lasers, and 360-degree projections challenged typical consumer perceptions.

RESULT HIGHLIGHTS | This six-hundred-guest event generated unprecedented attention from the press and won a slew of industry awards, including the Grand Prix at The Drum UK Event Awards.[19] Buyers from both big-name stores and smaller independents described the event as the best

19   Ishbel Macleod, "UK Event Awards: inVNT Scoops Grand Priz for Miele: The Science of Perfection, November 28, 2014, https://www.thedrum.com/news/2014/11/28/uk-event-awards-invnt-scoops-grand-prix-miele-science-perfection.

product launch they'd ever attended, by virtue of the awe-inspiring approach to product presentation. Within just 48 hours of the event taking place, unit sales had already exceeded the twelve month forecast—gains that more than paid for the event itself.

STEP 4 | DEVELOP THE IDEA. Telling a powerful story in the live brand experience space requires evocative, emotionally relevant creative components, key messages, and a direct challenge to the audience that's grounded in the consumer behavior the client seeks to change. Audiences are really, really smart. They've seen a lot—and they show up at an event likely convinced they've seen it *all*.

Is it great to open an event with a marching band? This kind of idea happens a lot, and generates an immediate surge of excitement in the opening stages of a brainstorm. Who doesn't love a parade? But if it has nothing to do with our Killer, if it's unrelated to the strategic imperative or our confirmed objectives, then that blood-stirring marching band is an example of starting with a tactic as opposed to the strategy. And so, the steps keep us in check. The question always has to be: "Is that right for this?" And the eye-roll test always has to be in play.

We call it *purposeful creative.*

Concept development is where all of the crucial information we gathered during the discovery phase coalesces, only this time we're asking *ourselves* the questions: How do we engage? What story arc will resonate emotionally, not just generally, but for this specific audience?

We work with the concept of "three headlines." These are the key takeaways that allow us to change the way our audience will think, feel, behave, and perform™ as a direct result of the experience. These headlines inform our call to action. In our process, a CTA doesn't have to be literal or transactional—it can be creative and subjective. For a Microsoft project we had audience members write postcards to their future selves, to be mailed out at the six-month mark post-event. This creative exercise was engaging in the moment, surprising in the delivery, and emotionally resonant, steering way clear of "been there done that."

DEVELOP THE IDEA | PEPCITY
BEST PRACTICE | LET'S NOT COMPETE.

PepCity was a refreshing activation amid a sea of
sports-themed Super Bowl experiences.

When tasked with the Super Bowl activation for PepsiCo, we knew we'd be competing with dozens of other megabrands to capture fans on Super Bowl Boulevard.

Deciding not to compete launched us out of the stadium and onto a different wavelength. We built PepCity as an arts and entertainment alternative to the countless sports-themed activations throughout New York City. By recusing ourselves from a crowded field we allowed unique variations on the sports theme to bubble up, from a rap battle between two talented hip-hop artists spitting football-themed lyrics to a celebrity-chef tailgate, with PepsiCo products as featured ingredients (the Cherry Pepsi–infused bacon was off the chain).

RESULTS HIGHLIGHTS | With lines all the way down the street and over thirteen thousand visitors, PepCity was deemed a spectacular success by PepsiCo senior executives.

Over 1,400 Instagram postings and 7.5 million Twitter impressions ensured that attendees became not just participants in the experience, but powerful brand ambassadors for PepsiCo. As citizen journalists, they shared real-time experiences across their personal networks: the most powerful form of advocacy there is.

> *Everything's possible with time and money.*
>
> **–Scott Cullather**
>
> *… but you only need one of 'em.*
>
> **–Kristina McCoobery**

DETAIL THE TACTICS

STEP 5 | DETAIL THE TACTICS. We lead with yes, striving to be a "Yes, and" partner, a practice that Kristina mastered while studying at Mason Gross School of the Arts. That means perceiving the production process as fluid, and never forgetting that we're an extension of our client's team. We're putting on a show, not pulling down the moon.

"Yes, and" means if it's going to increase the budget, we let them know, but we do it. If a client's unexpected request is going to delay the event, or relocate it, or the talent will have to change, we design that solution, lay out the cost implications, and let the client make the decision. We never assume the client's not going to want to spend any more money or delay the process. We never tell ourselves that if we avoid the issue entirely, maybe the client will have a change of mind and the whole thing will just go away. As far as we're concerned, having a knee-jerk, negative reaction to a client request creates an issue of its own, which is an erosion of goodwill. Those repercussions may not be felt right away, but they'll weave into the very fabric of the relationship. "Yes, and" are words to succeed by.

In our world, there is no such thing as a challenging client. Each client and every project is a teacher. When we hear younger team members complaining about how challenging a client is, we swoop in with an adjustment—as emotional leaders, we want to encourage our team to avoid the express train to martyrdom and self-pity. Not that any business is the place for those attitudes, but ours certainly is not.

The preproduction "nitty gritty" isn't just an equipment list; it's the detailed orchestration of staff, creative elements, and audience experience. When we staff a project, we're not focusing on availability—we're looking at fit. With the goal of servicing and executing an idea flawlessly, we construct the best team for the project, readily combining staffers with freelancers and scanning our global tribe for the right players. It may happen that a team based in San Francisco brings in a tech client, but because the parent company is based in New York, our NYC team takes the lead on production. Or, when a CEO is based in London, our London team shoots the video even though other elements of the campaign are being produced stateside.

As production schedules and timelines are being tracked in weekly or biweekly meetings with all stakeholders, we remain accountable to the earlier steps. Of course, we're focused on budget and schedule, but the Killer remains alive and well.

DETAIL THE TACTICS | SHRM ANNUAL CONVENTION

BEST PRACTICE | PLAN, PLAN, PLAN—AND WHEN YOU'RE DONE PLANNING, KEEP PLANNING.

With its many moving parts, the SHRM Annual Conference, with over eighteen thousand attendees, requires meticulous attention to detail.

The Society for Human Resource Management (SHRM) has an important reputation to uphold within the industry, which means the stakes are always high for its flagship Annual Conference. All in all, the conference attracts over eighteen thousand HR professionals who attend for development, education, fun, and to gain tools and resources to help their companies succeed. Each year they are treated to a packed schedule of general and breakout sessions, and an impressive roster of highly coveted A-list speakers and entertainers. Managing all four general sessions, the overall show flow, including the timing and coordination of keynotes, performances and interviews, required rehearsal, rehearsal, and more rehearsal.

RESULT HIGHLIGHTS | SHRM's post event attendee survey revealed a high level of enthusiasm, with 85 percent of first-time attendees planning to recommend the event to a friend or colleague, many commenting on how much they enjoyed sessions led by Brené Brown and Blake Mycoskie, and audio/

video production value bubbling up as a key driver of the event's success. The SHRM Annual Conference 2019 was featured in 882 media articles with a combined reach of 100.6 million, with the ad equivalency value of this exposure calculated at $994 million. The #SHRM19 hashtag trended during the opening general session, delivering a total social reach of 18.3 million during key dates.

STEP 6 | DELIVER THE EXPERIENCE.

In live production, there are no do-overs. No matter what you've prepared, something is going to happen that you haven't thought of. The weather. The talent is late. The audience is in a different state of mind or emotion than you expected and hoped. The venue has problems. Out of nowhere there is negative press about the product about to be launched. The unforeseeable complications are endless. You need three or four lines in the water—a Plan B and a Plan C and a Plan D—because you don't know what's going to hit first. But you can bet something will.

Let's say we're at a venue and we're building a contingency plan in case something goes wrong with the on-stage screen. We can't just rely on the vendor bringing us a new one. We need to know where the next available screen can be found, the resources for repair, and how we could replace the whole darn thing with a different model.

Theater craft is at the core of what we do: strong actors are prepared body and soul. When something goes wrong, a trained actor can improvise in character. We strive to know our material cold—the layout of the space, every executive entrance, every light cue—so much so that we're entirely "off book" and don't have to look at a piece of paper. With that level of preparation, if something goes sideways, we're so much more fluid in our response because the show is ingrained in our collective body.

With preparatory strength and improvisational ease, we don't need to wait for a debrief to hear about something a client would have preferred to go differently: we're ready to honor client requests in real time, and nine times out of ten we can adjust whatever it is. These moments aren't ass pains—they're opportunities to make the event better, to make ourselves better, and to strengthen our client relationship.

That being said, a central philosophy to our training and our on-site presence is "own up to it—immediately!" In real life, things go sideways, and nothing is more real life than a live event. If it's wrong, it's on us. In the case of a rare screwup, we do not delay, do not hide, do not throw someone else under the bus. We do not say it was the vendor, and we most definitely do not say it was the client. We own it, apologize, and move on.

DELIVER THE EXPERIENCE | ATLANTIS SANYA

BEST PRACTICE | DELIVER AUTHENTICALLY AND LOCALLY.

A team of over five hundred from six different countries brought the Atlantis Sanya launch to life.

With an execution team of six hundred, and a core team of twenty people from six different countries, our local Chinese crew and talent were an absolutely essential resource.

Our client wanted to celebrate the launch of its first Atlantis resort in China with a unique experience that would position it as a must-visit destination for both domestic and foreign tourists. We recognized the creative theme of "duality" in this new relationship between Atlantis and China. From there, we developed a theatrical east meets west experience. Recontextualizing the Greek myth of Atlantis, we wove in Chinese mythology, costumes and talent, and cast Jane Zhang, "the Celine Dion of China," who walked out to a thunderous standing ovation.

RESULTS HIGHLIGHTS | The award-winning event was attended by an international audience of over eight hundred journalists, influencers, and business executives, and the global live stream attracted over two million viewers who were eager to get a first look at this impressive new resort.

Heiko Schreiner, Atlantis Sanya's managing director, was incredibly pleased with the experience, noting: "It was a momentous opening celebration befitting a leisure development of this size and scale."[20]

STEP 7 | DEBRIEF AND PLAN FORWARD. At the end of a project, we review, assess, and report on performance with two separate and equally critical debriefs. The internal one, designed to help us prepare for our client debrief, comes first. Here we can safely assess as a team where we might have fallen short and where we can improve. It's also an opportunity to celebrate our wins and reinforce the talent and skill that made them possible. It's entirely possible someone on the team faced a challenge that is likely going to come up in the overall debrief with the client: here we can further our mentoring efforts and demonstrate both accountability and transparency.

For the client debrief, we're proactive about assembling an agenda that goes out well in advance, so that the client team can add their own items. We consider honest feedback, not a love fest, to be the purpose of our debrief meeting: we want to do better, we want them to come back to us for another round, and we are interested in developing our relationship.

The debrief process keeps us honest. We may have produced a wildly successful show that got great feedback, and everyone's ultimately happy. So, who wants to go in and talk about the moment when there was a video glitch, or a frayed temper, or not enough

---

20   Media OutReach, "Fosun International unveils Asia Pacific's first Atlantis Resort in Sanya, China," April 29, 2018, https://www.media-outreach.com/release.php/ View/5413/Fosun-International-unveils-Asia-Pacific's-first-Atlantis-Resort-in-Sanya,-China.html.

vegan options at craft services? But we will bring these details up, even if our client doesn't. What this rigorous honesty does is add credibility to our team. Accountability deserves respect, and it earns respect. Typically, it also defuses a potentially tricky situation almost immediately.

We bring in our metrics, our scope of work, and our *Comms Brief,* and we evaluate our performance along every step of the project from contract award through the end of the execution. And not just our own—the client's roles and responsibilities, too, with the goal of creating best practices. As difficult as it is, it's important that our clients also understand where they succeeded or fell short. If we were dating during the discovery phase, now we're married. The respect is there, the commitment is there, but the gloves are off. We arrive at true creative and executional intimacy, and in our experience it's an absolute requirement of a long-term, successful partnership.

DEBRIEF AND PLAN FORWARD |
SAMSUNG GALAXY NOTE 8

BEST PRACTICE | ACCOUNTABILITY
EARNS RESPECT.

The debrief was key to our ongoing client relationship with Samsung.

It was a first-time client, headquartered in South Korea, a massive product launch, and we'd ousted the incumbent. So many, many things went right … but not all of them.

The debrief was key. We went in openly and honestly. Admitted that we'd been unprepared to manage the volume of people who showed up at the same time. That there had been language barrier and translation issues. That our recommended venue proved to be a tough spot, resulting in cost overages. In short, we presented what happened, owned it, and laid out how it could be improved the next time.

RESULTS HIGHLIGHTS | Renewed business is the ultimate vote of confidence. We won the next two product launches and successfully delivered on our promise to resolve the issues that arose during the previous event.

TAKEAWAY: DON'T ASK FOR DIRECTIONS— USE A MAP

We invite you to help yourselves to our tools. Whether you apply or adapt ours or develop your own, your clients, your team, and your brand deserve a flexible but consistent road map. You don't want your success to feel like a fluke or lightning in a bottle. You want to deliver results, time after time, and build credibility and repeat business. If you don't know where you're going, how can you get there?

CHAPTER 6

PERFORMANCE CONTENT AND THE BIG POWER OF SMALL DATA

> *Storytelling works because it's brain science.*
>
> **–Chris Hercik, CEO, HEVĒ**

W e're living in an era where well over half of the world's population of over 7.7 billion people are millennials and Gen Zers who'd rather have an experience than a "thing," and who want digital as much as they do live. Brands that want to engage this enormously powerful demo must create amplification. Without digital, live isn't nearly as amplified. But live is the content that matters. These platforms are two sides of not just the same coin, but *major* coin.

When it comes to consumer insights and data collection, live events are already the most potent form of intelligence gathering on target audiences, because they're essentially captive for a period of time without interruption. These days, effective live events powerfully demonstrate the *phygital* trend—thriving at the intersection of digital platforms and physical points of sale, experience, or relationship. With live, we know what they're seeing, feeling, and hearing. They're not behind a computer screen, closing out a banner ad. We *have* them, and while we're communicating, we can capture the data. But our strategic relationship to data gathering is changing radically, and the businesses who get with that program are going to win.

The fact is, while our live event ideas are consistently disruptive, memories can be fleeting. We need our clients' experiential conversations to stay relevant long after the big moment fades into memory. At INVNT, we know that *the next level of live must take its cues from digital*, where the science of predictive analytics is already generating future insights with a significant degree of precision. "With the help of sophisticated predictive analytics tools and models, past and current data can be used to reliably forecast trends and behaviors milliseconds, days, or years into the future,"[21] as business-tech journalist John Edwards puts it.

Leading edge content development channels analysis of viewer behavior and preferences, demography, and household income to deliver detailed strategic considerations. With data-driven strategy, digital content both reflects and reaches its audience with an unprecedented degree of insight and accuracy, and the myriad aesthetic— and financial—choices that go into content production and distribu-

---

21   Edwards, John. *What is predictive analytics? Transforming data into future insights,* CIO, https://www.cio.com/article/3273114/what-is-predictive-analytics-transforming-data-into-future-insights.html, May 16, 2019.

tion are no longer a matter of pure aesthetics and gut: they're brain science. Today, brands can show up already knowing, for example, that time-lapse photography and black and white formats outperform closeup, overhead, and POV shots, that the talent should keep her hair down and straight, as long hair outperforms short and curly hair in studies of the target demo, and when featuring product closeups, the talent should be wearing a silver ring and violet nail polish. Predictive analytics leads to naturally high viewing time and ultimately saves our clients media money. When their audiences find the content based on actual brain science, brands will be spending less on paid advertising and promotion, making the meaningful connection that Lucie Greene, Worldwide Director of JWT's the Innovation Group, calls "decentralized, personal, and visual."[22]

Accordingly, we're not just preaching the predictive analytic gospel: we're investing in it, with the launch of our dedicated story studio, HEVĒ. Established in 2019, HEVĒ is housed within INVNT and specializes in narrative-led, innovation-inspired, data-fueled "Performance Content" designed to deliver higher levels of engagement and value for brands and organizations. At the helm is two-time Emmy and three-time Webby award winner Chris Hercik, an established master of the data scrape as the essential strategic tool of content development. Based in New York City at INVNT's global headquarters, HEVĒ is a collaborative of creators, strategists, innovators, and producers, combined for the first time with the latest in predictive analytics.

HEVĒ uses algorithmic formulas to leverage over 220 million minutes of video that's been tagged with a variety of relevant meta data points, like ethnicity, gender, place, time, color, celebrity, and

---

22   Lucie Greene et al., *The Future 100 2019,* J. Walter Thompson Intelligence, The Innovation Group, p. 2.

non-celebrity. We get super specific (e.g., "Tell us everything we need to know about women, ages thirty to forty-five, who like DIY videos."). From that question, we learn about all the videos she's watched the whole way through. We'll learn what products she's engaged with, down to, for example, her favorite yogurt brand and flavor. With her viewing behavior in hand, we begin to design our creative, which we continue to analyze using the same tools. From there, we gather suggestions and make "microedits," adjusting every detail from product shots to the color choice for on-screen graphics.

Today, we think about digital impressions differently: they're as plentiful as stars in the sky and, frankly, just as scattershot—it's engagement that matters. And to get completion rates up, you need to produce content that viewers actually want to watch. Today, with HEVĒ on hand, when a client asks us why we think something's going to work, we show them data points that support the *why* of both our recommendations and their investment. (Reality check: Reminding a CMO that color choices have been vetted and analyzed scientifically, rather than arbitrarily, may or may not nip backseat driving from Video Village—or Monday morning quarterbacking—in the bud. But you'd miss those conversations if they were gone forever ... right?)

Today, we're in the process of transferring that established digital process to the live event experience. Because for live to continue to evolve, we need to apply the power of measurement. HEVĒ's mission demands that every event we produce be supported with discovery content that leads into the event, thought leadership content during the event, and "momentum content" coming out of the event that's designed to continue that story long after it wraps.

With HEVĒ fired up, we stay nimble. We avoid the dense bureaucracy that comes with the traditional agency model. We avoid a degree of cumbersome demographic study. We're still able to come in, sit down, and listen—*really* listen—to what a brand has to say and discover the core emotional need we can address. The beating heart remains human as ever, but the live experience approximates immortality, carrying real weight and leaving long-lasting, visceral connections. With data to support the why, HEVĒ's prediction models enable our creative teams to understand with 90 percent–plus accuracy how an event, video, or campaign will change the way target audiences think, feel, behave, and perform™, before it ever runs.

TAKEAWAY: SMALL DATA > BIG DATA

There's so much chatter about "big data," and how it defines our times. But for the purposes of live brand storytelling, big data can be overwhelming. Nobody knows what to do with it or how to process it, or even where to begin in asking the right questions. HEVĒ curates small data—defined by brand expert, author and *Time* magazine Influential Honoree Martin Lindstrom as "seemingly insignificant consumer observations that completely transform the way businesses are built and run" as the DNA of our concepting.[23]

---

23   WSB, "Martin Lindstrom," accessed October 14, 2019, https://www.wsb.com/ speakers/martin-lindstrom.

CHAPTER 7

MAKERS' DOZEN

E arlier on, we shared the discovery process we undertake with clients—a considered series of "whys" that leads us to the core need, which in turn becomes the seed of creativity, innovation, communication and growth—INVNTion.

At the very core of INVNT are a "Makers' Dozen"—a can't-fail toolbox of twelve universal ideas and practices that we believe can be applied successfully to any endeavor, whether that's harnessing the power of live to build a brand, developing your team's capabilities, starting your own business, navigating your career inside a large organization, or just effectively inventing your future.

1. **PERCEPTION IS REALITY.** Success is a direct result of perception, and we're in the service business. Our reality is our clients' perceptions, full stop. However they've perceived our performance, that's how good it was. If we give ourselves an A+, but the client hands us a B-, that's our grade. There's something freeing in this philosophy,

because it holds the possibility that it's "not always us." On the other hand, professionals (and grownups in general) simply must learn the humbling art of surviving an ego blow. If a gap opens up, if we did a really good job that for whatever reason didn't translate, we tell our teams: "Don't beat yourself up." But the fact is, now we're dealing with the clients' experience, and whether we personally agree or not is frankly irrelevant. In these cases, we get to shift into solving the issue and changing their perception, then move on.

2. **WE ARE NOT A CULTURE OF "I, ME MY."** The most successful organizations are collaborative. If you're going to have a collaborative environment, you have to excise selfishness from your mind-set. Selfishness in this case means looking at our contributions in terms of what we can get out of them, and how they can serve our own ambitions, rather than how we can give to an inclusive effort that benefits the whole. Here's a simple practice that can illuminate where this tendency lies: before hitting send on a team email, scan it for the word "I," and consider how the tone of the entire message would change with replacing that single word to "we."

3. **KNOW WHEN TO LEAD, AND WHEN TO FOLLOW.** Basketball greats Michael Jordan and Scottie Pippen are pure examples of this dynamic. What Jordan did brilliantly was understand that giving Pippen the opportunity to lead would create a strategic advantage. In every team, and within every collaborative success, there are natural leaders and natural followers. But sometimes the leader needs to

make space for a follower to step up and lead in order to build consensus and enthusiasm across the team.

4.   **ACTIVELY LISTEN.** Listening isn't a reflex. It's a learned skill. We can't talk and listen at the same time, but active listening is even more than simply not interrupting. It requires compassionate, respectful focus and a deep sense of curiosity, which in turn allows for thoughtful response. Response is not reaction. For most of us, when we're supposedly listening, we're in fact formulating our reaction and waiting impatiently for our first opening to serve it up. Reaction is all about "fix it" mode. It's about "What are we going to do, and how do I save my ass?" Whereas response is about: "What does this other person need?" Yes, we're in the service business. But before we activate our fix-it function, active listening is where we build deeply felt and successful relationships with both our colleagues and our clients.

5.   **BADGER YOUR WAY TO THE SOLUTION.** We're fans of millennials and Gen Zers. Simply put, they are wicked smart. They're tuned in to pop culture. They're digital natives, and quick with everything. In other words, they're assets across the board. On the other hand, they come out of the womb with an iPhone in their hand already connected to Google Search, which allows them to take a keyword and within seconds their task is done. Except when it doesn't, and it's not. At which point so many millennials and Gen Zers hit a wall and roll over dead. Some challenges require taking it to the next step, and then the next step, and then the next step, all the way to the finish

line. (These were skills taught to Gen X and boomers at the library, where to find the book you'd have to hunt dimly lit stacks with a piece of paper in hand, on which a ridiculously long call number, found through the Dewey decimal system, was written with a golf pencil.) Stonewalled? Probably not. It's awesome to be tech savvy. But when you let it diminish your grit and perseverance … that's bad for you, your brand, and humanity in general.

6. **BE SPECIFIC; ANSWER THE QUESTION.** Fat in communication is rampant. It's irritating, wastes time, and creates uncertainty. Each word needs to tell: give 'em the center cut. Make the question specific. Be concise. Brevity communicates confidence. Make the answer specific, too. A specific answer to the question "What's the temperature outside?" can be "It's seventy degrees." A common answer to that question is: "It's seventy degrees now, but there's a chance of rain, and when I was listening to the news I remembered this thing that happened, and I had a feeling about it." But all we wanted was the temperature. We don't have time for whatever that was. And now we're confused; that was a full menu of different messages. We're uncertain, too, about the information as well as your emotional maturity and confidence. Do you really have the right answer, or are you bullshitting? Remember that old saw, "Less is more?" Still true. (PS: Precise communication is a great benefit of active listening.)

7. **IF YOU WANT TO BE A LEADER, START THINKING, BEHAVING, AND ACTING LIKE ONE.** Sure, there's a lot we can say about the myth of work/life balance, the

truth of work/life blend, nonbinary identities, and the state of personal privacy in the Information Age. But aspiring leaders still need to conduct themselves as such. A jackass selfie on your Instagram page? Flipping the bird? Dropping F-bombs? Just, no. The first thing anyone is going to do once they meet you is Google you, then shoot you a LinkedIn invite. If you're an employee, at INVNT or anywhere else, your behavior is on the clock at all times, even if you're telling yourself you've unplugged. Want to be a leader? Try that shoe on that feels five sizes too big (we referred to it earlier) and start growing into it.

8. **DREAM BIG, IT'S MORE FUN.** Don't let yourself settle for one little studio shop with three people. Let yourself picture building the next Microsoft or Samsung. Yes, if you dream big, you could fail big. But if you shoot for the moon and fail, you could still get to Everest. Allow yourself to dream. Allow yourself to explore what you really want and to picture it in Technicolor detail and begin to translate that idea into daily actions. Dreaming never hurt anybody. (But people who never allow themselves to dream often do.)

9. **WRITE IT ON THE WALL.** What do you want for your business? For your client? For yourself? Identify it. Paint a picture. Keep it front and center so that you're constantly reminded of your own vision, can notice quickly when you deviate, and effectively get back on track. You have to know where you want to go if you are going to have a shot at getting there.

10. **YOU HAVE TO GO THROUGH WHAT YOU'RE GOING THROUGH TO GET WHERE YOU WANT TO BE.** Setting the goal is the beginning. Then comes figuring out how to do it, or what the next immediate step could be, and putting your head down and doing it. In an organization that supports individual ownership, that could mean working with a manager to chart a course. Or reaching out for informational interviews or other connections with people in the department where you see yourself. But even if you're in an environment that's not supportive, you can still accomplish what you set out to. Swimming upstream, baby steps, starting somewhere, putting one foot in front of the other ... all of these, separately or together, can still get you there.

11. **DON'T BE AFRAID TO ASK FOR HELP.** Asking for help—not a bailout, not a handout—is the opposite of weakness. It's actually a great strategy. Look for help from the best—from the people who are knowledgeable in the areas you want to grow. Sources of help can be guidance, counsel, emotional support, networking/introductions, or the review of materials and the giving of notes. When you ask for help, your humanity, vulnerability, and integrity shine through, and those traits are often attractive as well as an aspect of the healthiest kind of leadership. Asking for help welcomes talented people in and inspires their investment in your success.

12. **SOMETIMES, YOU'VE GOT TO JUST PICK UP THE PHONE.** We can email. We can text. We can Slack. We can Zoom. But sometimes, we just need to pick up the phone and say, "Hey. Listen. Here's what's going on. I

need to pick your brain." It's always amusing (and occasionally wildly infuriating) to ask a team member to give someone a call, and then wind up on the cc list attached to the email they sent instead. One of the perils of technology is the loss of that personal connection, coupled with tonal ambiguity. You can choke the whole operation with smiley-face emoticons, but they will never replace actual warmth or professionalism. And for sure, these frankly avoidant and sometimes lazy practices dilute the power of true verbal persuasion.

One of the great dichotomies of our business is that we know millennials and Gen Zers are hungry for shareable experiences and live interactions, and they're brilliant at imagining and producing these on a massive and meaningful scale. But they'd rather fire off a text than walk down the hall and talk to the person. Ease with these key human capacities is still key to professional growth and success, and we believe it always will be. To manage a team, or build a business, or lead an industry, you have to know how to get in the room and sell the idea. You have to give verbal feedback in uncomfortable situations. Every single day.

It's a big, colorful, crazy, intense, imaginative world. The stakes are high. And in this complicated world we share, there's no substitute for genuine dialogue. There's no substitute for a firm handshake. Or, our absolute tried and true favorite, eye contact. Because when it comes right down to it, when two people connect, when their molecules mingle in real, can't-make-it-up life, that's the ultimate live event.

Now get out there, Challenge Everything, and blow shit up. (But first, call your mother.)

Kaboom!

FIRED/ACQUIRED/
FIRED/REACQUIRED

> *You have to go through what you're going through to get to where you want to be.*
>
> **–Kristina McCoobery**

E leven years after cofounding INVNT, we still live on the Upper West Side of Manhattan. Our apartment's a little bigger than it was back when INVNT headquarters was our dining room table. Our three fantastic kids are in college or on their way and are preparing to launch: fingers crossed for a successful liftoff.

In 2015, we sold the business to Time Inc. and sailed away on a solar-powered catamaran to the Maldives, where we are cultivating an artisanal vineyard.

Okay ... that artisanal vineyard bit's a crock.

What's true is that in 2015 we sold INVNT to Time, Inc. What's also true is that two short years later (or endless, depending on how you look at it) we bought it back—by the skin of our teeth.

And in that two-year window, a sometimes exhilarating, sometimes harrowing stretch of road, we grabbed the brass ring, swung from it with aplomb, rode out a major reversal, found our footing, and, as of this writing, have a store of wisdom to share with those who want what so many entrepreneurs do: to lovingly and tirelessly build a global brand—and then sell the heck out of it.

Thankfully, we didn't do any of this alone. Blessed with solid counsel and support, we leaned on it heavily. We were particularly helped by a tried-and-true business process model, yet another brilliant brainchild innovated by John Wringe, our London-based Nonexec Chairman. John shared his model with us early on, so we always knew we were growing and evolving in line with this model: it synthesizes the learnings of his long and storied career into a "life cycle road map" of successful marketing communications businesses. At our core, we all experience similar ups and downs, but this model allows us to predict when they are more likely to happen, so that we can plan ahead. And while it's not a forensic plan and there's flexibility within it, the four key phases of John's model—survival, establishment, deal, and succession—were certainly apt in our own experience and infused our process with both strength and perspective. With a keen sense of how things were likely to go two steps in advance, we were far better prepared when our airtight concept of exit strategy didn't play out the way we thought it would. (One prominent left turn was the discovery that Andrew Bernstein's law firm, Mintz Levin, the same one that helped set up INVNT on day one, had a conflict of interest and couldn't represent us during the sale. Kristina reached out to Gregg Gilman, from the prestigious law firm of Davis and Gilbert, who'd represented Kristina when we were forming INVNT and famously advised her: "I don't know who this Cullather guy is, but you deserve a better deal." All those years later,

Gregg was there for us when we needed him, negotiating a great deal on the "in" and an even better deal on the "out.")

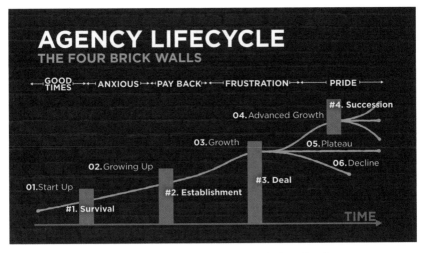

The model enables us to predict and plan ahead.

Remember: We'd been invested in the idea of smartly engineering a wise and profitable exit strategy since our Williams/Gerard days, when Scott had approached the elder statesmen who'd given him his start with big ideas about how best to pass the baton. (You may also remember how well that went. And how the ensuing hot mess sparked the creation of INVNT.) As we created and built our own agency, the goal of selling was always part of our mission: unlike the professional culture we'd come from, we wanted our roles to have concluding chapters as energized and well-designed as their debuts.

So much for big ideas.

We were looking for the Holy Grail, and instead what we found was a door. To get to that promising threshold, we had to go through some incredible shit. Here's what happened (or … what our attorneys will let us tell you).

Five or six years into INVNT we had interest from several private equity firms. Despite the presence of enthusiastic potential investors, we weren't ready to sell; we knew we hadn't built up enough value in the business. And then, in 2014, we received a call from an investment banker that got our attention. There was a seriously interested potential buyer who wanted to get into the live event space. And not just any buyer: Joseph A. Ripp, a former CFO of both Time Inc. and Time Warner who'd become Time Inc.'s CEO in 2013.

Scott wasn't just late for his first meeting with Joe. He was twenty-of-the-longest-minutes-of-his-life late, having gotten stuck in traffic, without Joe's mobile number, and arriving at a swanky, subdued restaurant in the Time-Life Building breathless and sweating through a formerly sharp navy blue suit after a six-block sprint in a heat wave. Completing his first impression look? Fogged glasses.

"Mr. Ripp's table is over there; he's been waiting for you" the sympathetic maître d' indicated. Talk about a live event: Scott approaching the table, hand outstretched to greet Joe, Joe's Chief Revenue Officer, Mark Ford, and the banker who introduced them, Wilma Jorden. Of course, Scott was mortified, off-the-charts stressed, humble, hopeful, and eager to get through this part and settled into a groove.

"I'm so sorry," Scott simply said. "My mother would not be very happy with me right now."

"Sit down," Joe laughed, seemingly unbothered and good-humored, "we're going to have a good conversation."

It *was* a good conversation, followed by several more, over cold martinis in a dark Irish pub. Joe picked a quiet, safe space in which to share his vision and his strategy to fulfill it, far from the relentless prying of Emily Smith's *Page Six* or Keith Kelly's *Media Ink*, the *New York Post's* infamous columns which constantly had Joe in its crosshairs. Time Warner, then worth $63 billion, was Time Inc.'s parent. Time Inc.'s print business was ailing, and Joe's strategy was to spin out Time Inc. as a stand-alone publicly traded company with strong financial prospects. Time Inc. housed many great print properties, and Joe wanted to extend them into the live space, following in the footsteps of its *Time 100* and *Fortune Most Powerful Women* events.

Joe saw what we did in the rise of millennials and Gen Zers. He knew that a robust live experience had the power to bring Time Inc.'s brands to meaningful life for the most important consumer demographic on the planet. We all felt the synergy: not only did we share a perspective, but we had many professional relationships in common, too. From that common ground, Scott felt comfortable sharing one of his main concerns with Joe: that Time Inc., with its massive scale, would squelch our ability to grow the business. But Joe dispelled that worry. Rather than make INVNT work like Time Inc., he was planning to set a compatible course, and assured Scott that he needed to change his business to be more like INVNT.

Like we said—that was a good call to get.

But of course, we weren't the only agency that Joe had on the line. A strenuously competitive vetting process followed. This was the dog and pony show of our lives (and we'd been to more than a few). Cocktails had led to a full-on capabilities presentation to Joe's team, and from there to his board. We poured everything we had into telling our story: INVNT came out of that ringer in first position. We were understood as a strategically relevant asset that would lead the transformational process Joe and his team had been tasked to execute. In 2015 Time. Inc bought INVNT one hundred percent.

INVNT was acquired by Time Inc. in 2015.

The deal closed with a life-changing number, and, because we had granted stock to sixteen of our seventy-five employees (another aspect of our vision forged during the Williams/Gerard years), made a handful of INVNTrs overnight millionaires. The stock element is very important to understand. After all, Time Inc. was buying a service business. Yes, INVNT has a proprietary methodology that works, and that can be successfully applied beyond its purview. But what Time, Inc. was really buying were those sixteen senior people in the company with skin in the game. Their vested relationship to the business all but ensured that they'd stay, stabilizing the transition. As is typical in these transactions, we'd remain tied to the business for an industry-standard period of time with an opportunity for an earnout.

Although we hadn't yet signed the deal, we were super close. Scott invited Joe to present at our company annual meeting as a surprise, having our employees sign NDAs in preparation for his big announcement. Kristina met Joe at his car and escorted him inside: we were brimming with excitement. When we made the announcement, the cheer that went up raised the roof; this was a moment of pure validation and enormous possibility. Joe, one of the most inspiring, visionary leaders we have worked with, spoke to our team and then the CEO of one of the most iconic media brands in the world humbly opened the floor to questions.

"Why INVNT?" someone asked.

Without skipping a beat, Joe answered: "Scott." He then went on to explain how Scott and his team's presentation represented the talent and efforts of the entire operation. Of course, Scott wasn't a solo act. We had an incredible leadership team, and our CFO, Wolf Karbe, in particular, was hugely invested in making the deal the success that it was. But it was Joe and Scott who had been dancing for months. It had been a long journey, well-played on all sides, culminating in a great deal. What's important about Joe's answer is that it highlights the key to a sale, and that's the culture and mission of a business, as embodied by its top leaders. In any agency sale, those irreplaceable personalities are rocket fuel.

On that auspicious morning, standing among our esteemed colleagues and watching them revel in the culmination of many collective lifetimes of effort, we were reminded of the importance of personal accountability, of showing up personally and individually for every transaction over the course of a career—even with fogged glasses. Just about every person in that room sweated the small stuff on the daily. We were a group that believed it was truly worth it to care day in and day out about the details *and* the big picture. Man, was that a moment.

But the earnout piece never materialized. And why is that, you might ask?

Because things changed. In mixed company, we call it a transition, based on "directional differences." Living through it was a far less tidy experience.

In short, not long after the bubbles had settled in the champagne and the cheers had quieted, Joe's print-focused team was out, and a new team was brought in, with a focus on digital and just about zero interest in investing in a live event business. And so, we began to necessarily navigate the unwinding of our relationship. This process, we assure you, was not for the faint of heart. A deeply difficult year followed, as our team became stuck in an endless, bureaucratic quagmire. Used to running and gunning, making game-time decisions, and spending as necessary going here and there, we now confronted the daily slog of numerous layers of approval for every move we made: at that point we knew we needed to buy our agency back. As the deal was being hammered out, the process snagged on two points: working capital and managerial oversight. That snag opened up a seemingly insurmountable gulf, into which the deal tumbled. And soon we were in a new round of negotiations.

At this point, we could have left all our toys on the floor and sailed off on that solar-powered catamaran. But our hearts were involved. Our company was made collaboratively, by great people who took a leap of faith with us. People with families that we'd watched grow up. We weren't going to let them down—not without a fight.

The new round of negotiations demanded a twenty-one day purgatory, in which we were no longer under the Time Inc. deal, nor were we in our seats at INVNT. That compressed window of time was nothing short of brutal and served up a slew of tough lessons. We learned what we were made of, as individuals and as a couple. Under this extraordinary stress, we learned about our team. We had loyalists who pledged themselves to our cause and whatever venture we'd undertake next, even if this one fell through: one of our creative directors, for the benefit of the many Time Inc. employees cycling through the office during our purgatory, replaced the framed wedding portrait on his desk with a photo of us, labeled *W[hat] W[ould] Scott and Kristina Do?* We had the diplomatic worker bees, people who avoided the fray, kept their heads down, wanted to stay employed, and thankfully kept our slate of projects on track and successful. Their even-keeled work ethic benefitted all of us enormously and produced a new crop of leaders. And, we learned, there were opportunists in the mix. While others had our backs, they were quietly placing targets on them, perceiving a land grab on the horizon. (They're no longer with the agency, duh.) Scott announced he wasn't going to shave until we got the business back, and soon was sporting a Santa-Claus-Meets-Forrest-Gump beard. We had to create a holding company as part of the process, which we aptly named Fury Events. It felt like a battle, because it *was* one, and it wore us down. Eventually, right toward the very end, when we were a single "t-crossing" away from getting our agency back, Scott finally lost it. He screamed at our attorneys, hung up on them, and retreated to the rooftop balcony of our weekend home to cool off. Kristina followed him upstairs to deliver good news, but Scott was still simmering. He hollered at Kristina and launched his wine glass off the roof. Finally, as Scott was crawling among the sea grass and hydrangea, retrieving broken wine glass shards, it occurred to him: "I've become

INVNT's reacquisition hit the industry news headlines.

Colonel Kurtz." (As in, the deranged army officer, felled by his own psychological warfare and portrayed by Marlon Brando in *Apocalypse*

Now.) Scott offered Kristina a heartfelt apology, along with some flowers from the garden: they agreed that Scott would no longer be allowed on any more phone calls with attorneys.

With uncertainty and speculation at a fever pitch among our team, somehow, we got to the other side. What we hadn't expected and would never have predicted: the acquisition was a smart idea, but the reacquisition proved to be even smarter.

Our acquisition, and then reacquisition, carved the way for INVNT 2.0.

We scheduled a company-wide call, gathered the tribe, and announced that we were getting the agency back. As you can imagine, there was enormous excitement and collective relief. This was the very same day that the Subway Annual Convention was loading in. Karmic timing, as Subway is our longest client relationship, spanning over thirty years. When we got to the hotel in Orlando, our entire INVNT team was waiting for us in the lobby, wearing pirate hats.

INVNT's current logo – aka tribal mark – encapsulates the agency's challenger mentality.

We christened this new era "INVNT 2.0." Taking all of the good stuff from the first era of the business, chucking out the stuff that had become obsolete, we hit reset (hello, slick new company logo!) and got into supercharge mode, accelerating our growth to

$54 million in turnover in 2018—and targeting over $65 million in 2019.

The fact is, our swing on the fired/acquired/fired/reacquired pendulum was essentially textbook. It's not unusual for sales to implode, for new corporate kingdoms to be installed at the eleventh hour, rendering promising alliances null and void, or for good guys to lose their shit and throw wine glasses. Our experience was a powerful teacher, about the value of diversified skills and roles within business (and personal) partnerships, the importance of collaborative leadership, and an uncomfortable truth, which is that business decisions cannot always be made by democracy.

We are so not done here.

As the industry that's shaped our lives is at the precipice of radical new growth, prominence, and innovation, we have so much more to do, say, and contribute. We are passionate about helping entrepreneurial service-driven ventures like ours create their brands, navigate hypergrowth, build IP, and get to that sale (keeping in mind that the brass ring often turns out to be a door handle).

> *You can dream big or dream small. Dream big-it's much more fun!*
>
> *And when you dream big your story has a shot of becoming legend.*
>
> **-Scott Cullather**

Cheers.
Scott & Kristina

INVNT's Scott Cullather and Kristina McCoobery.

ABOUT THE AUTHORS

SCOTT CULLATHER

CO-FOUNDER AND CEO, INVNT

A recognized industry leader, over the last thirty years Scott has led teams in the design, production, and execution of hundreds of large-scale B2B and B2C brand experiences in over forty countries, for dozens of the world's leading brands, companies, and trade organizations.

KRISTINA MCCOOBERY

CO-FOUNDER AND COO, INVNT

A passionate and proactive mentor, Kristina has over twenty years of industry experience. Along with overseeing the award-winning agency's operations, she manages some of INVNT's largest accounts and longest-standing clients.